The Book of Last Resort

A Subversive Guide for Artists in the Digital Economy

By Jon Reed (he/him)

Foreword By Rachel Meyers

About the book - and book credits

Published by eCruiting Alternatives, Inc.
ISBN: 978-0-9725988-7-3
Available retail from Amazon.com
Available wholesale from Ingram and its subsidiaries
Available free on many online e-book platforms
Audio version will be available free on podcast platforms

Content edit by Rachel Meyers
Interior design by Rachel Meyers
Print-ready formatting: AtriTeX Technologies

Back cover café photo by Andrea Burns
Cover design by Keith Draws
Foreword by Rachel Meyers

Note: the use of the Garamond typeface is consistent in all my books, dating back to my first self-published book, guided by my beautiful departed friend and mentor Michael Doane.

Contents

Dedications

This book is dedicated to Paul Dykes – one of my Booker T. Washington. English teachers from the legendary BTW English wing. Mr. Dykes corrupted me with a glimpse of my creative possibility, and just in the nick of time.

I would also like to thank the Booker T. Washington. class of 1986. Who would have known that decades later, you'd light my way forward. Speaking of which – Beth, I hope this book lives up to what you ignited in me so long ago.

Thanks to the current and graduating students of my alma mater, Hampshire College; you put this material to the test in workshop sessions. Special thanks to Carin Rank and the Hampshire College SPARC team, who believed in this content. Oh, and to my far-flung *Valley Optimist* colleagues, Yes, we "did our stint to get our name in print," and then some.

As for the rest who got me across the finish line, you know who you are, starting with my mother. My colleagues at diginomica are the reason this book exists at all. Jonathon Podolsky became the friend that kept me from the pandemic abyss. Beyond that, there are too many of you to mention here, but you are never forgotten.

Foreword

When I first met Jon Reed, it was in the heady, early days of the dotcom boom. As IT recruiters for an online headhunting agency (before Monster.com, before Indeed), we were on the cutting edge. You couldn't *not* make money. It was easy to think we had it all figured out.

But something was amiss, and Jon would not stop talking about it. Creativity was being supplanted by success. He was haunted by writing projects he hadn't finished, guitar lessons he hadn't practiced enough for, creative endeavors he hadn't even started. He was longing for a different existence, one that centered on his creative self. That longing was terrifying. And contagious.

From Jon's perspective, yes, we were successful – we were even creating a boatload of online content – but something needed to change. It turned out that change was coming, whether we wanted it or not. The dotcom economy collapsed. Vulture capitalists swooped in and destroyed our bubble, as they did across the industry.

This seismic shift rocked our world. We were forced into the reckoning; embracing new opportunities was the only option.

One of those opportunities was writing a book based on our humorous experiences as headhunters, *Resumes from Hell.* While the book never achieved commercial success, the story of our book got picked up by local and national news outlets. Our 15 minutes of fame culminated in me doing a 6-minute interview on CNN. The thrill of that alone fueled the writing bug for me. What else could I write? Did I have another book in me? Could I be a *writer*?

These were questions I toyed with, but for Jon, they felt like life and death. "Success" by 30 should have felt like he was winning, but the projects he had been back-burnering for years nagged at him.

It was during these days, when we were redefining ourselves after the dotcom bust, that Jon really started articulating the concepts you're about to learn. Jon was contemplating his creative future with a protectiveness and ruthlessness that I hadn't seen before. He was in an existential struggle to correct his course. His creative pursuits were going to take a front seat, and it might get ugly. It *did* get ugly.

Jon was re-evaluating everything. Work, friendships, relationships, family, his free time. Everything was viewed through a new lens: did it help or hinder his creative self? Could a friendship survive if Jon stopped going to movies with that person because it cut into his writing time? What if he missed their birthday party? Their *wedding*?

Even Jon's artistic endeavors were re-evaluated under this harsh light: was he good enough at guitar to keep taking lessons? Was a blog good writing practice, or a vain distraction? Was he willing to abandon the content that paid his bills? Did he have the courage to submerge himself in his fiercest, most personal writing?

What I didn't know then was that Jon was testing out the theories and methods you are about to read in this book. Jon was reclaiming something that was already his: the creativity that defined him. It was the ushering in of a new era. Jon's creativity was ready to take up space again. He was going to take a chance on himself, embracing the power of his potential. His goals shifted from commercial success to creative fulfillment.

The Jon Reed I met 25 years ago would be proud of the Jon Reed I know today. Today's Jon is relentless in his pursuit of the creative. He writes, creates, tests, reflects, tinkers, and is in the fight every single day. He is no longer dissatisfied and yearning. Instead, he is creating and producing. No matter how absurd and complicated life gets, Jon is loyal to his creative self. Today's Jon will go to the grave knowing he gave it everything he could.

How did Jon get to the point of creative liberation in the fray? By using the methods laid out in this book. In the pages that follow, Jon is going to ask you to do hard things. He's going to ask you to create, share, endure criticism – and then go back to the drawing board. He's going to ask you to question anything that doesn't support your artistic endeavors, including friends, relationships, free time, hobbies, and social media. He's going to ask you to shut down your phone, stop doom-scrolling Twitter, and filter out the noise. He's going to ask you to make tough decisions: abandon what's not working, be honest about your innate abilities, and test the limits of the people you love. He's going to ask you to cut out the dream killers, whether they are jobs or people. If that sounds uncompromising, it is. But it is the only way to ensure your creative redemption.

Jon wouldn't ask you to do anything he hasn't done himself. He has done all of the above and more. In the most extreme times of his life, he calls these sacrifices "giving blood." He will show you that giving blood may drain you and test you, but it can also save you.

Over the past 25 years, Jon's methods have intrigued, terrified, and then inspired me to do my own version of the same. Jon lives in a way that makes you question yourself: your motives, your goals, your decisions. He lives by example – a code, even. If you are someone who thinks about your creativity and fulfillment and what it all means, you can't help but compare your journey to his. Are you willing to sacrifice what he has? Do you have what it takes? Are you able to be brutally honest with yourself?

In light of these questions, I forced myself to give up on what wasn't working – specifically, two writing projects that were so misaligned with the reality of my writing abilities, that they languished for over a decade. I had to ruthlessly examine myself before I could let go. It wasn't pretty, but it was necessary in order to evolve. I had to admit – to myself and eventually, to others – that most of what I was seeking was that validation from the CNN interview. When it came to writing again, I didn't have the moxie or the discipline, only the vanity.

But in facing the failure of those projects, there was a gift: space to pursue a career and spiritual ventures I was better suited for, and breathing room to build my legacy in other ways. I tore down the shrines (both literal and figurative) to those dead-end dreams. With emotional space cleared, I had room to do a mid-life career pivot to publishing. I am now finally exploring the endeavors that will fulfill me and be my legacy.

None of this would have happened had I not had Jon, always orbiting nearby, testing and pushing himself to his limits. His journey inspired mine. His proximity held my feet to the fire. His methods influenced major decisions in my life.

Now, reader, it is your turn. There is a reason you picked up a book called *The Book of Last Resort.* You may be disheartened by fear, dread, exhaustion, or your lack of creative productivity. You would probably rather die than live an unfulfilled life. *But you are not defeated.* You have decided to correct your course. You are ready for an unsparing pursuit of your own excellence. You are ready claim your creative voice, out on that path of no regrets.

The book you are now holding may be the most important book you ever read. If you relate to Jon's story, if you feel that same urge to reclaim your creative self, I urge you to keep reading.

In the pages that follow, Jon will show you how to build creative muscle and build discipline. He will beseech you to seek out criticism and risk failure. He will urge you to get on the treadmill of trial, error, and output. He will show you how to strive for mastery by giving away your best work until you've built an audience and can monetize.

Ultimately, he will ask you to take a chance on yourself. That will mean taking risks, narrowing your focus, and getting out of your comfort zone. It will mean sacrificing lifestyle addictions. It will mean moving towards the darkness and risking exile. It will mean protecting your creative edge as though your life depends on it. In all the ways that matter, it does.

I hope you will be as inspired by Jon's musings and methods as I have always been. Let him be your guide through the darkness. He has done it. He *is doing* it. And you don't need to go it alone.

Get ready to be "a brave and terrified badass."

Rachel Meyers

Preface – This Is Your Book of Last Resort

If creative fulfillment eludes you, read on.

This book is what it says: a book of last resort. Most will not care to read it. But if you're an artist suffering without clarity, maybe it will matter.

By suffering, I mean you feel trapped, unfulfilled. Your day job is corrupt or all-consuming – or your finances are breaking. Your relationships are either unsatisfying, drama-drenched, or non-existent. Or maybe your relationships are wonderful – but a part of you resents the people you love, for luring you away from creative work you never found a way to consummate. You're boxed in by a life that doesn't reflect your gut potential.

If you're cursed/blessed with creative drive, you'll never solve that unless you wrestle these monsters down. If you're reading this book, you already know this, somewhere in the pit of things. You're alienated from the creativity that would define you.

If only you could channel that bittersweet into the creative expression that would change the terms of your existence! Maybe even get you paid for the fruits of your unconventional toil.

Perhaps I missed your exact predicament. Point is: if you're reading *The Book of Last Resort* – shit ain't workin'. A life of fair payment for truthful expression eludes you. The badass inside you is stymied by a tight or white collar.

When you lose the freedom to express your truth in all its raw defiance, your creative spark fades. Too many artists are paid to do a Coors Light version of themselves. Yep, that pays bills. Until it dawns on us: the marketplace carved us.

Most of us didn't set out to sell out. But when we try to outwit circumstance, maneuvering the rent and then the mortgage, small concessions add up to surrender. *We are playing the wrong game.*

The Book of Last Resort is just that – a book you turn to when others fail. Yes, other books whispered sweet comforts in your ear. "You can unleash your creative genius." You can "find the artists' way." Just "do what you love, and the money will follow." But they left you with an impotent feeling after the "4-hour workweek" gimmickry fell short.

That book is now at the tag sale; the creativity guru is twenty bucks richer times thousands, and you're drinking the vinegar of your disappointment, that sinking feeling your life doesn't matter – at least not the way you envisioned when you were young and unmitigated, and your dreams hadn't pushed back at you.

Not the way you burn for.

If you burn to create, *The Book of Last Resort* is for you.

We're all more creative than we give ourselves credit for. But are we all artists? My last book, *Free From Corporate America*, was basically for everyone. It was for creative types who lacked financial savvy. It was for business peeps who lacked creative inspiration. *Free from Corporate America* is the book I wish I had in my possession when I graduated from college, humping between crapjobs with a ludicrous frame backpack jammed with minimum wage uniforms.

This book is different. It's not for the many. It's for those who deign to call themselves artists, despite the risks that come with such pretensions. I'm not going to exclude anyone – if you're in, you're in. Define art however you want. If it works for you, you qualify. This one's for the freaks and geeks, and whoever the shoe fits.

Ideally, we would all be creative in how we live. Thoughtful parenting might be the ultimate creative act. But I define artists as those who are driven to create legacies that live on. Artists are those who scrap (and scrape) for those moments of poetry you can only achieve in the flow of expression – the ultimate act of FU against the mundane.

Artists persist until that defiance adds up to a sculptured product – archeological inspiration to the outliers who come along later. Just like when we read Camus, listen to Aretha, or stare at Dali.

The best art is an alchemy of fierceness, longing, and unforced creative perfection, pulling us into the moment while taking us beyond it, like Jimi Hendrix in "Little Wing" or the culminating scenes in *Apocalypse Now.*

Even if you're a relentlessly devoted artist, you may never hit those peaks – but you'll happily squander your life trying. That means moving beyond tattooed hipsterism into ass-busting creative product. And doing it again and again, long after the tattoos fade and the groupies find a preferable idol (or idiot).

If the gods smile upon us, our creative output may generate an economic return. But that was never the urgency behind our creation – though artists *do* crave an audience, however small, that will walk through fire with them.

So does parenting qualify as art? You could make that argument. My teaching years convinced me parents shouldn't take as much credit – or accept as much blame – for their children as they typically get.

No matter. If raising children makes you an artist, I'm not qualified to help. Being the best parent you can be is laudable. It's also out of my scope. Besides, there are classes for that. There aren't classes for what you're about to read.

This is *The Book of Last Resort.* If you're a parent and you're reading this, an elusive *something* is still missing – however chaotically full your life might be. Something is lost inside you; something is restless – and even the affections of family can't make it right. I live that wrongness when I unload on someone who deserves better.

Resentment betrays a void of authenticity, a knot of thwarted self-expression. *You are not aligned with your fate.* Obligations are mounting. That gnawing feeling: time is running out.

So you are here. For a scorching 200 pages or so, you are with me. You're ready to face some hard truths along the way, because that is the price of a ticket you yearned to pay your whole life.

Embrace Your Subversive Creative Power

If you're heading anywhere as an artist, you must embrace your need, no – your craving – for power. The shrill warning that "power corrupts" is absolutely right, so danger lies ahead.

But there is another risk: lingering in powerless obscurity. I am here to tell you: you are supposed to be great. *You are supposed to shine.* You will be a monster inspiration to some. You will threaten the bones out of others. You can't worry about either. They are sign-posts on the road you must partake.

If you have any ambivalence about power, *you are not ready.* Before we can proceed, you *must* be willing to soak in excellence. *You need to take up space.*

Here's why power gets a bad rap: people cling to institutional status for material needs. More often than not, it's a suit that doesn't fit, a boat anchor on their destiny. They typically abuse that power in the process of running away from themselves.

I get why you wouldn't want that kind of power. As Fleetwood Mac sang, might be better to put your kingdom up for sale. Let others pursue power for vacant, narcissistic ends. You're not one of those. But that doesn't let you off the hook.

True power is earned, not granted. *True power is created by manifesting your uniqueness.* The power to ignite a spark isn't given to you. You can't inherit it. You can't coast on it based on reputation. *You have to fucking seize it. You have to create it. And then you have to keep earning it, over and over again.*

Here's the most terrifying/wonderful part: that power doesn't come from strutting your talent. It comes from alchemizing your pain and loss. *It comes directly from your scars.*

Too many artists think they can avoid the power conundrum by lingering on the fringes. According to this tired ethos, you should be selfless; you should renounce the ugliness of power-seeking ambitions.

Rejecting power doesn't stop you from hurting others. You hurt others by clinging to skin that doesn't suit you, seething inside like an interpersonal time bomb. You hurt others when you opt for silence over fierceness. You hurt others when you diminish the implications of your own possibility, and, by extension, theirs.

If you're resistant to claiming power, let me run this definition by you:

> *The power to manifest your creative ideas in the world. The resources to bring ambitions to reality. The means to help others launch their subversive pursuits.*

Oh, and this:

> *Achieve your relevance by providing a transformative experience to those you inspire. Do it through your guts or your mastery – and your triumph over adversity.*

I use the word triumph cautiously. Adversity comes in two flavors: external and internal. I'm not sure we ever triumph over our internal demons. Maybe for a day, a week, or even a very good year, but those demons have a way of coming back strong. To put it another way: we are born flawed. Carrying those flaws with grace is a lifetime process.

"Triumph" speaks to those kickass moments when we summon creative work into the world, despite all that. Think of Joe Biden's inaugural poet Amanda Gorman, stunning the crowd at age 23, the youngest poet in history to do so. Yeah, that's a huge triumph. But peaking like that doesn't mean your struggles are over. The real triumph isn't a fleeting moment of glory: it's overcoming *anything* that prevents you from planting work on the wall. Maynard Keenan of Tool usually doesn't face the audience when he performs – perhaps the moment is too personal. But yeah – he can sing. He turned that overcoming into a discipline.

If you're not ready to shine, you're not ready for this book. If you're not ready to infuse your creative work with the truth as you see it – no matter how difficult or taboo that truth might be – then you're not ready. Put the book down; come back when you are.

Who the Heck Is Jon Reed?

Now that we're past the power thing, who the hell am I to talk to you like this?

The answer: I'm nobody. But yes – I've used the principles in this book to tangible effect. I'm not a famous artist – far from it – but I'm not promising you that anyhow.

I started this book in my mid-40s – I'm 54 now. I've run my own business for about 20 years. Despite years of humbling effort, I'm not much of a guitarist. My drawing skills are oceans from gallery-worthy. My video skills are reluctantly improving; I hope to be active in film someday. After loads of practice, I'm a pretty good podcaster. But I can write. I've worked at it and fought with it for a long-ass time.

Beyond reams of blogs, I've published three other non-fiction books. Officially, I'm not a published fiction author yet, but I've done more fiction than I'm ready to talk about. Spoken word isn't something I do often, but I've had my moments.

Blogging/podcasting/video advanced me in the tech field. Perhaps I understate: it's put a roof over my head, invoked life-changing adventures, and changed my circumstance. My creative output in that field has reached a niche global audience. But here's the kicker: I was in a career pickle, *until I employed the subversive tactics you're about to read.*

Since then, I've built a number of web sites powered by my own content. Some failed; some shifted my tectonic plates. Some that failed changed my life the most.

My life is not without adversity – far from it. I'd like to think my existential struggle gives these words an authority I wouldn't have if I was kicking my feet up on an island, or hanging out with Beyoncé. You decide.

No, I don't hold myself up as a role model. Nor have I achieved the peak of creative excellence I'm talking about here.

But that's the beauty of it. You don't have to reach the pinnacle to see your life fundamentally change – *when you cultivate the right talents.*

I thought about waiting to write this book until I was truly "at the top." But that's not how life works. That final step – broad commercial success – is elusive, unpredictable, and bizarrely distributed. In the age of diminishing intellectual copyright value, it's tougher than ever to get there.

I don't think of myself as destined to live a long life. Most days, 54 feels like a miracle. So I decided: I could delay this book no longer. Yes, there are artists far more successful than me – but none of them have written this book.

Massive success brings blind spots that make "advice" hard to swallow. Most who hit the bigtime develop a self-serving mentality: "If you do what I did, you'll have the kind of life I have." It's fantastical bull-pucky – sorry Dave Mustaine, love you, mean it.

But as I leaned into this book, it dawned on me: portraying myself as another hard-luck dude on the fringes might not be very persuasive either.

If you apply what I divulge here, you can take things *an astonishingly long way* from where you currently are. You can do it your way – and hopefully get a lot farther than I did.

When I think about the lowest points in my life, teetering on a stadium ledge when I was 16 years old, staggering from a hit-and-run accident that should have killed me two years later, I am humbled by the damage I carry with me. How I'm still here is a mystery I'll never understand. I'm not gonna let you down and bury this book because I don't feel worthy.

In my own creative development, the things I needed to hear most were hidden by convention, and hard as broomsticks to find. I scoured used book-stores. I picked up scrapes and bruises as trade for my illusions. The used bookstores are long gone now, so you'll find a different map. The scars you'll need anyhow.

I'm not promising anything except for this: when you fight through the crapstorm life throws, when you hurl work that reeks of authenticity out the door, you'll feel more alive. You may even feel an unexpected peace.

By peace, I'm not referring to some kind of meditation guru quaalude nirvana. *I mean the quiet confidence of taking a chance on yourself when nobody else did.* When you're done with this book, you'll know how to manifest your work.

Manifesting is powerful. It brings clarity to your relationships, though not all of them will survive this magnificent unraveling – and that's ok too.

Commercial success is an algorithm. Some of those variables are beyond your control, but some of them are not. I'll ask difficult things of you to improve your chances. And yes, you can adapt these tactics to your professional life as well.

Read on, and you *will* claim your creative power. But your power is not absolute. It may reveal itself in peculiar, rather than earth-shattering ways. Sorry, this is not the path to riches. But it *is* the path of no regrets.

I'm not giving you some rehashed version of the American Dream; I'm not giving you the tongue-pierced life of a player. I'm giving you the truth, or as close as I've ever come to unvarnishing it. Hopefully it will spark something inside – something worth fighting for.

Before this slim epic you're reading now, I wrote the aforementioned *Free From Corporate America: A Practical*

Guide to Success on Your Own Terms (2009), or "*FFCA*" for short. *FFCA* is a prequel to this one, though you can read it afterward as well.

Free From Corporate America is the book I desperately needed after a very mixed bag of a liberal arts education – and didn't get. It's for anyone affected by the outsourcing/automation economy, as long you don't mind a sprinkling of profanity, and the occasional chip on the shoulder.

Where *FFCA* can help is putting theories from this new book into practice. *Free From Corporate America* takes a hard look at how you get yourself launched when you literally have no time, and maybe no money, and feel completely strapped by circumstance. There's a load of content in that book on manipulating time, and tactics for getting projects off the ground when time is scarce. *FFCA* also gets into the specifics of creating income-generating assets. I will not repeat that here.

You can get the full "special edition" audio version of *FFCA* on podcast platforms for free, performed with abandon by professional narrator Bill Laing. And you can get the e-book version for free pretty much everywhere too (except Amazon, which forced me to charge for it. More on that paradox later).

Free From Corporate America skewers formal education, retirement accounts and investing, resumes, and even home ownership.

One more thing *FFCA* gets into: the specifics of financial management, in an unconventional way that frees up the most important thing – your time. Money in the bank matters little if you're scampering 'round the hamster wheel.

Before we press on: don't let the artistic examples in this book put you off. I've called out a range of artists that inspired me, but I left out plenty that deserved mention – like one of my local heroes, Dave Houghton of Fancy Trash, whose jugular performances taught me so much about musical possibility. I erred on the side of the unsung, hoping readers might get the fringe benefit of welcome discoveries. I keep making them, as in my recent discovery of next-gen bluegrass alchemist Billy Strings. I asked this book's editor, Rachel Meyers, to insert a few favs that I missed. I hope our examples remind us: on the way to finding our own rhythm, we must seek out our predecessors.

Massive changes have ensued since *Free From Corporate America* came out in 2009. Unfortunately, most of them impact artists head-on. One is the dominance of social media, which all artists must grapple with. In the original version of *Free From Corporate America*, I cracked a joke about mySpace. That gives you some idea of how far we've come. In some respects, not far at all.

The Social Noise Threatens Our Creative Endeavors

I don't think too highly of social media for artists. I see too many creatives losing their rhythm, circling a dysfunctional Instagram rabbit hole. Or, their work comes out mediocre, because mediocre work (sometimes) gets plenty of Facebook likes.

FFCA does point you to the Internet's invaluable feedback loop. The Internet forces a dialogue between you and your audience. That holds true today – though that dialogue is veering towards useless memes of late.

You think Led Zeppelin would have made a decent album if they brought their mobile phones into the studio, getting pinged whenever their besties posted baby pictures? If the Beatles were sweating hostile Twitter feedback, would they have found the stones to tape their experimental masterpiece, *Abbey Road* (e.g. "get rid of the medley; that's whacked!")? You think Pink Floyd would have benefited from checking LinkedIn while recording *The Wall*?

In today's hyperconnected world, we must come up for air more often. It's hard to pull off a year of studio isolation. But the point stands: the crowd consumes brilliant content, but does NOT create it (try reading that horrible novel crowdsourced on Twitter sometime).

The other thing I did not anticipate in FFCA is even more grim: the declining respect for intellectual property. Yes, people still love to consume art, but by and large, they don't feel obligated to pay for it – with the possible exception of subscription-based streaming via the aggregators (Spotify, Pandora), trickling pathetic royalty streams to creators.

Today's consumers might be willing to pay a premium for "experiences" around the art they love, but that means you have to live on peanut butter in the back of a tour bus – or become a merch vendor, selling branded mugs and hipster hoodies. That's not what most of us envisioned.

Being an artist in a market economy was never a fun project. Now it scrapes. Oh, the digital krishnas will assure you otherwise. They insist the Internet creates all these amazing new ways of getting close to your audience. Of *interacting.*

There is that magical Internet word – "interacting" – aka "fan engagement." In the era of free, it's not enough to create art that moves people. Now you're expected to interact. A hermit like J.D. Salinger, content to stand on the merits of his work alone, would be pretty well screwed.

Your Creative Work Thrives on Free

Properly harnessed, the Internet is a potent distribution channel. But there's a bitter pill. You must let go of getting paid. At least not until you build a serious level of notoriety.

Your creative work thrives on free.

That's one of the least fun sentences I've ever had to type. If you make your work free – voila! The power of the Internet goes to work. Peeps will browse your TikTok videos; they'll read your short stories (or at least some of them, especially as you build followers). Even better: if they like your work, they will share it.

But they probably won't share your work if it isn't free.

Sharing things your friends have to pay for isn't perceived as cool. Digital networks thrive on free stuff. Especially on smartphones – folks just want to push play. That's why babies and kitties get fifty times more attention than your paywall-protected art.

Yes, micropayments on well-designed platforms like Kindle can work. But on Kindle, the best you're going to get is a good review, not a social share. "Free" takes the distribution of your work to another level. Crowdfunding and fan-supported sites like Patreon are gaining steam, and that's an encouraging bright spot. But for now, the hard truths beat out the easy money.

And: most Patreon folks *do* give the core of their work away. Mostly you give away the entree, and try to sell the sauce. Yes, that is changing for some – but usually those selling their latest work had to give something away first.

As I head towards publication, I'm seeing more examples of selling the creative entrée, and not just the sauce. Some examples come from podcasting. I've seen models of sharing an hour of a two-hour podcast – with more on a premium subscription. Or, a free/premium combo option. It's encouraging to see these models emerge, though most of these do include substantial free digital content to earn the initial audience. The paid subscribers stem from that.

There are other interesting pay-for-art trends, like email-based subscriptions for short stories (see Substack.com for one interesting example). *That's because it's not always about free.* A "frictionless micropayment" is the bottom line, if you don't mind choking down a techno-junkphrase.

It's all about consumers on a platform/app that's easy to use and to spend on, like Prime, Kindle, or Apple. That's another reason why Patreon is working – folks sign up, then add another service. It's easy to support multiple artists this way, with just one login. Whether you can make enough money on micro-royalties to put a dent in your obligations remains to be seen. That's all about the platform, the percentage you get, and how much you can sell.

That's why I come back to this: give your work away *until the audience is engaged, passionate, and subscribed.* Then you can look at how to monetize.

I do want to be clear though: you should never be pressured into giving work away you want to sell. You have an absolute right to sell your work, and control when it's given away. You alone should determine the price tag on all the public work you produce (just note that price tag is not the same as value, no matter how much you charge).

Fortunately, you don't have to give all your creative juice away (I'll get to that). But if you burn to be an artist, be prepared for the enormous collective appetite for free content, or it will rip your intestines out, and with that, your fortitude.

I don't condemn people for wanting to consume art on their own terms. Consumers have proven they are willing to micropay or subscribe for convenient streaming on platforms they like (e.g. Kindle for books, Netflix for movies, Spotify for music, the *New York Times* for news). However, I'm not sure they realize that "what I am willing to pay" does not necessarily add up to what the artist needs. Then the great art is threatened. Creating exceptional art is usually a byproduct of significant time and production expenses. Tossing up a YouTube video of a band rehearsal is a different matter. It might resonate, but the chances of it being exceptional are slim.

Whether creative micropayments represent fair compensation for creative consumption is the nagging question. For all but the most popular artists, I lean towards no. Either way, micropayments aren't going to help you anytime soon, and they may never help you. Same goes for YouTube advertising revenues, where eyeballs don't add up until you're in the millions of views.

YouTube finally seems to be catching on; though it made a harsh change in the algorithm to downgrade the value of subscribers, it's also added creative monetization options, such as "joining" a channel as a paid subscriber, or paying to have special visibility in live chat streams.

Some artists claim to love micropayments because the only cut is to the aggregator – Apple or Amazon or Google. No greedy agents or exploitive/incompetent record labels. But you have to sell a heck of a lot of product to put micropayments at the heart of your business model. And you are dependent on the whims of massive/amoral content aggregators, tweaking the algorithms that control who finds your content – whenever they feel like tweaking them.

Micropayments are a hard road. The emerging model of paid subscribers – direct to the artist or via Patreon-type sites – is the more encouraging route. But you must earn the audience first – and that's where "free" is (usually) non-negotiable.

"Free" Isn't Defeat – It's About Using Digital to Build an Audience

As of this writing, book authors have a better shot than musicians of proving me wrong. The economics of self-publishing on the Kindle are significantly better than Spotify. But the terrain of the aggregators is constantly shifting. These days, it's an advertising game on Kindle, less than a free game (you pay to advertise your book series and make money, perhaps, from there).

Either way, "free" is either going to be the wind in your sails, or the blowback that knocks you on your dejected ass.

Dig into Chris Anderson's book on the topic, appropriately titled *Free*. It was published in 2009, but a big chunk still applies. Be warned: Anderson won't advise you as an artist. He is way too infatuated with how content aggregators like Google used "free" to build empires than he is with helping you. But Anderson's context may help you figure out where to drill your fishing hole.

Free isn't just a price point; it's a way of consuming digital content "without friction." Charging for content erects barriers between you and your audience. Yes, peeps will climb those barriers if you write *Harry Potter* or *Game of Thrones.* They'll climb if you are Radiohead or Rihanna. Otherwise, they'll just consume something else that's free. Or they'll find your bootlegs/mashups/pirated stuff. Or catch your latest concert via phone footage on YouTube, whether you granted permission to film or not.

The era of free brings an entitlement mentality to intellectual property. Yes, proponents of free claim they are willing to pay – *if* you make the price reasonable and the content easy to consume, but that's not the guts of it.

Most consumers believe the greatest gift they give to an artist is their attention – and sharing your work on their social stream. They (wrongly) assume their collective attention is enough for you to monetize.

Yes, if fans fall hard for your work, they might be up for paying for an additional "experience," like the aforementioned concerts, limited edition t-shirts and book signings – who knows, maybe a belt buckle. I go for beanie caps myself.

Piracy is one expression of that entitlement. Fans will post recordings of your performances; they'll copy and paste your work into forums, mix your music into a club jam, with or without express permission – usually without. This is all considered fair game by a surprising amount of fans.

If your art is embraced, your most likely "compensation" is a modicum of celebrity. Then you have to figure out the rest. The Taylor Swift level – where you monetize every time your cat gets a hairball – isn't likely, so you'll need a different plan.

Niches Cut Through the Noise

Here's a more realistic goal: name recognition in a smaller niche or sub-genre. But that doesn't necessarily translate to income either. I learned that the hard way, waxing poetic about forgotten hair bands. It led me to epic adventures, but not to money.

Some self-published writers give away books on Amazon, win a genre fiction audience, and charge for additional books in a series. Once readers are hooked, they're more likely to pay. (Note: Amazon has opaque rules for how books are offered for "free"; it's too brain-freeze-complicated to get into here).

Micropayments can work, in those rare cases where the genre interest is big enough to scale. For plucky fiction writers on Amazon, that could add up to a decent living in genres like detective, science fiction, vampire, or erotica. It must be specific enough to fascinate you and reflect your identity, but broad enough to be classified with similar titles – that's the genre dance.

If you can shoehorn your art into an established genre, it *will* help. Anderson's book prior to *Free* was *The Long Tail*, a book that inspired naive sycophants to blather about how the Internet enables us to reach audiences of one (or a few), deep in their niche.

That's partly true – the Internet enables you to "narrowcast" your work to smaller groups than ever before, and to do it across geographies. No matter how taboo or edgy, there's a subculture out there that will consume your stylings. Whether they will pay for it is another matter.

Digital consumers expect affordability. Unless you are creating high-end collectibles for an affluent audience – as some visual artists still do – *The Long Tail* won't do much for you financially. The only long tail winners are the familiar suspects: our pals Amazon, Apple, and Google, aka the aggregators.

The long tail *might* do something for you emotionally. Hearing from someone in Iceland who groks your stuff never gets old – but you can't take that to the bank.

Take the movie industry: as studios scramble for the rights to *Spiderman* spinoffs, there's a vanishing middle class of creative work. *Ordinary People*-style "adult dramas" that once won best picture don't even get funded. Huge blockbusters get the nod. With the right connections, you might get the greenlight for a low budget bootstrapper.

Alas, regardless of creative discipline, the vanishing middle class of artists holds true across the board. You're either wildly successful or scrambling these days, with the possible (rare) exceptions of self-published genre fiction, or musical touring workhorses.

Pretty much any comic book you grew up reading is going to become a movie, thanks to a risk-averse industry of rubber stampers. "Direct-to-Netflix" might be the only film development that's promising for creators. Or perhaps the surge in episodic subscription television.

Your early work might be brilliant, but chances are it will be imperfect. Genre audiences are forgiving. They are more likely to support your work while you are still shedding skin.

It's a damn sight harder to get paid for genre music than genre fiction. You'll probably need to give your music away, and try to make it up in touring and merch. In the timeless words of Henry Rollins, lead singer of punk legends Black Flag, "Get in the (freaking) van."

Yes, you may be able to audience-build by streaming on live channels. But whether the van is real or metaphorical, the point stands: sacrifices come before audiences materialize.

The Grateful Dead Didn't Fight Free – Neither Should We

For each art form, there is a way to make "free" work for you – rather than against you. Warning: when/if you decide to give your work away, don't just share teasers. You're gonna have to give away some peachy stuff. And you're gonna have to make your peace with those who rip, pirate, and unapologetically duplicate your hard-fought output.

Immersive stuff that moves people is hard enough to conjure; giving it away without resentment is harder – at least it was for me. Think of free content as the backbone of your marketing plan. And yes, all artists are now marketers by necessity.

The biggest blunder an artist can make is to fight against free. Try to monetize too soon – and fail. I've made that mistake, and I've made it bigtime.

Monetization is the final stage. Build your audience, build your rep, build a culture of loyalists and contributors around your work. Then see what's what.

Think Grateful Dead and how they embraced fans' bootlegs. They built monster tour followings, back when you had to swap those bootlegs on cassette tapes. That's the model of "free" artists need to study. Except: switch cassettes with the distribution steroids of digital file swaps, and Twitch streams. *Update: in a strange irony, I've learned that the Grateful Dead are one of the most ruthless enforcers of music copyrights on YouTube, even instances I'd argue qualify as fair use. Copyright is a complex issue; artists deserve to make their own calls here. Of course, for artists without fancy legal teams, it's tougher to navigate. I had to leave out a handful of notable song lyrics from this book; the copyright terms of lyrics are ultra-strict – I lacked the time and resources to try for those permissions.*

Anyhow, if you can pull off something similar to those old Dead cassette swaps; if you can build a culture around what you do – which sounds way more compelling than a "fan following" by the way – then you *should* be able to monetize. Just be prepared for that monetization to take a different form.

You may have to merchandise yourself. You may have to position yourself as a consultant. If you manage to bigtime it, you might have enough fame – at least within your niche – that you can revert back to what's left of the "old media" economy: sign a big film/book deal, get an agent to represent you, negotiate ridiculous contracts, and all those fun hijinks.

But, and this is a big-ass but: contrary to what the "Internet changes everything" snake-oilers insist, that's a spin of the roulette wheel. If you're clinging to the dream that you can huddle over your fiction like Salinger or Kerouac, wait for the world to track you down and compensate you for your eccentricity, while agents and brokers line up the swellest deals on your behalf, *obliterate that fantasy now.*

To pull this off, you'll need to master things completely outside your comfort zone. Learn to work a room, or even speak in front of it (yes, as Holden Caulfield might say, "goddamn Toastmasters"). That might mean booking – and pushing – your own gigs. The person most responsible for putting up your band flyer is *you.*

And yeah – as much as it irks me to concede the point – it *might* mean interacting with fans on Facebook. I'm not as social-hostile as I posture. I have no issue with social media for artists, as long as it doesn't undermine your one and only chance to change your life through sparkling work.

Building Platforms – Why Bother?

Solitude is a potent vehicle. If you use it well – not from the pit of despair but as a creative opportunity – it will change your life. In solitude, you excavate. You unearth what no one else could summon. Camp out on Facebook like everyone else; become like everyone else. Vanilla is contagious.

The time to use social networks is *after* you emerge from brave forays with something original. Professor/blogger Cal Newport calls this necessary process "deep work" – he published a book on that topic, titled, appropriately enough, *Deep Work*. If you pursue deep work relentlessly, it can change your career – in almost any field. But it's even more profound for your art.

Wading through that internal swamp forces you to unravel your riddles, surfacing creative work that's steeped in personal truth. Once that part is done, plunge into the external side – push your free/soulful content, and earn your audience.

You might need to build a content-rich web site that attracts the attention of a publisher, or some other benefactor. Or: a YouTube or Discord channel might be your main haunt.

That's what's known in the publishing biz as building a platform (not a technology platform, but a brand/distribution platform). The main ingredient in a platform? Easily-consumable, shareable content, usually backed by subscription lists to sign up for more.

Beneath that platform is some serious lifting. Others can help you polish and propagate, but only you can wrestle it from your soul. Even then, your work has just begun.

Unless you're the next coming of Alicia Keys, purge the "I'm an artist; my handlers will do the rest" fantasy. You can't just toss content into the wild. Your art will need a savvier/grittier push from you than that.

Yep, artists must get over their queasy feelings of self-promotion. One consolation: the power of free means that marketing will meet you halfway.

And that may be the best news of the free era.

This is where you, the shunned creative genius, suddenly has a big, modern advantage. Traditional "interruption marketing" of branded bullpucky is flailing.

Edgy/handmade/soulful content is winning – at least sometimes. *And that's something you can do.* Here's the kicker: *you can do it a heck of a lot better than the marketing suits can* – even if they have a degree in marketing and a big budget to blow, and you've got a shit sandwich.

Once I started giving content away, everything changed.

The more content I gave away, the better it got. Yes, I still loathe the entitlement of the freeconomy. And yes, I worry about the future of art, particularly the most financially intensive art, like music and film. I worry about the future of *All The President's Men*-style investigative journalism. I worry there will be fewer *Apocalypse Now*'s that took years and untold risks to achieve – and a studio with loads of faith in that artist to fund.

I worry there will never be another *Dark Side of the Moon*, or *Pet Sounds*, brilliant studio creations that would be disallowed as expensive indulgences today. Only artists with the deepest pockets and commercial track records have a shot at that funded freedom now.

I wrote this book as a side project, but not all art can happen that way. Some of the greatest art ever made requires immersion – and production support. You think the Beatles could have recorded *Sgt. Pepper's Lonely Heart's Club Band* after a long-ass day as Uber drivers? Films are the same. You can film *The Blair Witch Project* on the fly. Have fun trying that with *The Deer Hunter.*

There's less and less immersive art of that caliber, with the notable exception of HBO-style dramatic television, which is in a post-Sopranos golden era (for now). Those cultural dilemmas keep me up at night. I don't have answers. But I do know this: things worked out a hell of a lot better for me when I examined how the power of free content could help me, rather than keep me down.

As I create/share my way to better projects, travel adventures and paid gigs, my bitterness about "free" has lessened a bit. That grudge will never entirely dissipate, because I believe artists should be paid for their excellence. But I would have been ruined creatively and financially if I hadn't reconsidered free, not as a religion or creative utopia, but as a tactic I could choose to employ.

To Rise Above the Noise, Find Your Greatness

We live in an attention economy. The more attention you gain, the more "attention capital" you can spend. Attention is not the same as real currency – we must never forget that. But if you gain attention, you should be able to convert that (yucko buzzword alert) "mindshare" into something material you can use.

This isn't about manipulating social media with viral crud. It's about building an audience that has a genuine stake in your work.

If you're like me, you flirt with despair because social networks trivialize creation (see how your new poem does on Facebook versus someone's wet poodle).

Or: if social networks don't trivialize creation, they democratize attention by making it easy for anyone to "lifestream" and win eyeballs – even with fake news that breeds brainrot with every share.

It's no fun competing for attention with kittens – never mind parrots talking to Alexa. And forget about competing with baby goats – not even Andy Warhol would have stood a chance.

So-called "smartphones," with their eternal notification blasts, are a guaranteed immersion disruptor. When peeps are texting, uploading "I saw a bear in my backyard!" videos, or opining on Louis CK, *The Walking Dead*, or presidential absurdity, they are not consuming your content.

It's tough to lure smart phone addicts otherwise normal people into focused consumption now – even inside a theater or concert hall. People are tweeting at the television, texting at the movies. Even airplanes are becoming as distraction-filled as anywhere else, with in-flight Internet and *Big Bang Theory* on demand.

Yes, people might click on your work, but: unlike twenty years ago, when they might have been interrupted by fussy kids, now you can add fussy kids to a massive list of tech interruptions, including mobile alert absurdity of all flavors, most of which are not urgent – all of which distract from immersion.

Capturing attention is becoming a miraculous achievement. Tread carefully – this demoralizing realization can lead us down desperate paths, tempting us to up the ante with look-at-me behaviors, sensationalized content, shrill confessions from the bell jar, and other self-defeating gestures.

So, we have a grim-looking creative predicament:

1. People want to consume content either free or on the cheap, in their digital format of choice – with no payment friction.
2. Your "fans" lack the immersive time or willingness to concentrate on much of anything, much less your two-hour YouTube documentary.

Yes, peeps might read your short story while texting their pal. But when it comes to attention, immersion remains the gold standard – that's how hearts and minds are changed.

Here's your digital attention dilemma:

1. Chase attention via celebrity/cult of personality; or
2. Dive headlong into the guts of authenticity, and earn attention the hard way.

Yep, this book is about number two. And yeah, maybe with a dash of number one. But only a dash – that stuff is chili pepper.

In the good old "World Wide Web" days, if readers liked your web site, they'd bookmark you and come back for more. These days, they won't come back – too many social media distractions. Yep, there are ways around that – think email/app subscriptions for starters. Alas, my now-archaic advice in *Free From Corporate America*, "If you build it, they will come" – yeah, that doesn't really work anymore.

The Cult of Celebrity and the Attention Economy Crossroads

The attention economy feeds into a Kardashian-like obsession with celebrity for its own sake. There's a savvier goal for the artist: a dedicated audience, however modest, that responds to your most brazen work.

As an artist burning for greatness, you are at the eyeballs-and-clicks crossroads. There are three choices; none of them are a school picnic. Choice one: give up on your art, fed up with the superficial distractions people seem addicted to. By giving up, I mean you can make the best of your day job, or live off the grid as best you can, surviving in obscurity, your best work decaying inside you, or stashed in the digital equivalent of the family attic. That may sound fatalistic, but I know plenty who have essentially made that choice.

Your second choice is more alluring, but perhaps more diabolical: bet on your charisma and cult of personality. You can pursue celebrity through virality. I'm not gonna lie: there *are* some beautiful/lucky/

charismatic people out there who seem to coast from opportunity to opportunity, based on their "extreme" antics – and their undeniable knack for keeping Instagram hungry.

Their lives might have a Kanye West-like chaos to them, but they have attention. They have millions of followers on Twitter (as in Fox Sports' Skip Bayless, who morphed from journalist to polarizing TV egghead).

The cult of celebrity makes the freeconomy easy. Doesn't matter what you did to get famous; suddenly everything you do is interesting. Every time your dog needs a belly scratch, every time you bite into a sketchy burrito at Chipotle, someone out there is glued to your lifestream. You are open for business – and brand sponsorships.

Modern celebrity has a disheartening plethora of examples. These are the reality TV shortcutters, folks who became famous without mastering anything, except maybe the art of the crotch grab. I don't know how to help you with that – wrong book alert!

Personally, I see this type of celebrity as more grim than fulfilling, but the temptation is there: perhaps through social media superstardom, we can sneak around the toil. Like that clever/fantastically fortunate dude in Sweden known as PewDiePie who gathered a huge audience that loves to watch him play (and review) video games.

That brings us to the third fork in the road – the one I'm trying to charm you into taking. To have a chance at a creatively fulfilling life, *you need to master something.* Mastery takes time, unsparing trial and error, figuring out what resonates, and busting it out. Again and again.

Throw out the misleading modern feel-good-psychobabble of "you can do anything you set your mind to." A critical ingredient of true creative success is working within your limitations. One of the most extraordinary vocal artists of the 20th century, Billie Holiday, had a limited vocal range: just over an octave. It was the acceptance of that limitation that inspired her to push limits. She extracted everything she could do vocally in that context.

Mastery is hardly ever synonymous with virtuosity. And creative virtuosity is rarely what moves people emotionally. Billie Holiday mastered her craft in a fluid jazz medium that liberated her vocal authenticity. The result: 70-year-old songs that have not changed in their ability to evoke.

Once you master something, you should pick up momentum through so-called lucky breaks, and the power of connections. And yeah, in most fields. mastery means working your way up, e.g., starting as a key grip or gaffer in film production. Or maybe even the stereotypical bagel-fetching intern.

Whatever it takes to master your craft, through the "iterative process" of trial, error, and output – that's your obsession now. Glamorous? No. But the end result might be. If you achieve a rare PewDiePie shortcut, fine – but staking your hopes on shortcuts weakens fortitude.

Don't chase attention via celebrity. *Capture attention by being great.* "Be so good they can't ignore you," as Cal Newport extolled in his prior book of the same name. If you are exceptional, you can still break through the noise – enough to win the attention that will change your circumstance.

Think *Game of Thrones* on HBO, or *Breaking Bad* and *Mad Men* on AMC. It was all appointment (or binge watch) television, for a big enough audience to matter. Or HBO's *The Wire* – hardly a hit when it came out, now an underground legend that launched careers.

You don't have to create a TV epic; attention works on a smaller scale. I have colleagues who speak/write/publish to a comparatively modest audience. But it's enough to matter. Especially if your audience can't get anything that resembles what you do anywhere else. Or: if some of them will hire you for projects. *In this cookie-cutter age, there is a premium on well-honed uniqueness.*

Don't think of attention as an absolute state. Attention is an in-flux continuum. We don't need all the attention all the time. We just need enough of the right eyeballs, enough of the time.

So avoid the temptation of social media preening. We don't need to be in front of cameras with nothing to say; we don't need to release a sex tape and disown it later. We just need to specialize, hone our craft, and share as much hard-won creative product as we can.

The Social Noise Vortex Drowns out the Mediocre

No, peeps won't turn off their smartphones for your content, but they might ignore a few texts on your behalf.

They might even share your stuff – creating a culture around your work that eventually becomes a community, or at least a network you can harness. *You now have a "platform" for your trouble.* A strong platform raises your creative profile, prompting those who rejected your early manuscripts to call you back, with self-effacing mea culpas and contracts in hand.

I have colleagues who are frustrated because their middling blog posts are getting ignored. In the attention economy, average is a fail – unless you have a celebrity-level distribution platform. If you blog on a monster web site like *Fortune* or *HuffPost*, you might get a wide enough readership, even if your prose is mediocre. But it takes toil and connections to score that high exposure gig.

Content aggregators like Amazon or Google have an advantage. At the Google scale of aggregation, you can push mediocre content and succeed on long tail volume. But that doesn't do diddly for you.

You will not get ***the right kind*** *of attention without being exceptional.*

Not all of your work will be exceptional, of course. Some of it will suck. Free yourself up to suck! Failure isn't a picnic either, but you might as well enjoy it enough to laugh and learn. The goal of every piece should be exceptionalism. The reality is wherever it lands.

The social noise vortex drowns out the average. That rules out all but the viral, the extremely well-funded, the ass-kissy, and the exceptional (ass-kissy = share/inflict the blog post my employer's buzz-word-infected marketing team put out). Chasing viral is the stuff of Instagram influencers. Deep reservoirs of cash are beyond my scope. Ass-kissing we can do on our own time, at our own risk. That leaves you with the unsparing path to exceptionality.

But as an artist, you shouldn't want to be average anyway. *You should want to be transcendent.* That's why you are here.

You may never pull off a "Stairway to Heaven" or a "Fast Car"; you may never be Maya Angelou or Spike Lee. But that is okay.

Because you are willing to die trying.

That unflinching commitment will imbue your work with power – well beyond what you might have expected. Meanwhile, you strive for that superlative moment until all your will is spent. That brazen quest is precisely what is lacking in the commercialized preening that passes for art today. Your ruthless and transparent pursuit of your own excellence will spark your audience.

The imperfect body of work you leave behind is your perfect legacy. *It tells us how bad you burned for this, how much you overcame.* And guess what? You'll have plenty of "good enough" along the way. Good enough changes lots of things. Manifesting your work leads to brilliant adventures as you shed the skin of complacency.

The joy of publishing imperfect work is a triumph over the perfectionism that once encumbered us. It's a big ol' middle finger to the "you can't do it/you're not worthy" voices that haunted you into silence. And: you get better.

No matter how distracted people become, we crave stories that resonate. We need moments of unexpected insight, emotional connections beyond four walls. You can do that. It comes down to two incredibly simple/difficult things:

1. Strive for mastery until it becomes a rhythm; and
2. Be willing to give your best work away, until your audience is big enough to transform your options.

So fight towards greatness, embrace the messiness and share work as you go. Then you will cross a bridge to manifestation. On a good day, that crossing may even improve your finances.

I could stop writing now – that's the gist. But there are subversive things to say about the role of love and friendship, and practical secrets on shoehorning this into your day-to-day.

The World Craves Artists Who Did the Reckoning

Most artists find themselves on a long interior hallway with a stark choice: hate yourself because of your unflattering flaws, or harness those flaws into naked expression. I know plenty of young artists who aren't happy campers. They simply don't see a place for themselves in the world as it exists now.

Like most of you, I've been ridiculed for being different as far back as memories go. In some dark moments when I was utterly lost, I'm ashamed to say I dished it out also.

We make capitulations to normalcy. Not wanting to face the blowback, we take the edge off. We cater to family wishes; we present a stylized version of ourselves.

But the shame builds. When the world of commerce mocks your creative grasp, when your job carves a piece of you with every shift, it gets worse. You are timeclocked into conformity. Or you do the slow fade; medication helps.

Getting royally ticked off is better than taking it out on yourself. But take it from someone who's had an unflattering chip on their shoulder for decades: that chip is more of a handicap than a rebel badge.

I hope you have a revelation before you get too much gray on your head. That revelation? *Your wounds are the kindling for your creative fire.* Your scars are meant to be brandished.

This world craves people who have done the reckoning – though they fear them too. Embrace that love/hate with all the poetry you can muster.

Each time you up the ante on the uncensored spleen of your self-expression, you'll feel better. But how will others respond?

Most you care about will eventually accept it – but only when they realize *you are* ***never*** *going back.* If they don't get it, so be it. Life is too short to submit to the dead hearts. Even if you have the profound misfortune of calling those dead hearts Mom, Dad, Brother/Sister, Husband, or Wife. (If so, you are not alone, and don't lose heart. You can do this.)

I'm going to ask you to do some hard things for your art. I can't do that if you don't believe in yourself first.

I went into a tailspin after college. My liberal arts degree seemed impotent. The things I did for rent were a mockery.

Yup, that was me – trudging from bus stop to bus stop, lugging that frame pack. But I got a nice bonus from bagging groceries: it burned arrogance off my soul. I had a Bachelor's Degree in What the Fuck?

I was cursed with an unflattering case of entitlement on the one hand, and a flawed "education" on the other. Both would take years – and massive helpings of humble pie – to overcome. To be fair to Hampshire College, my alma mater, my Hampshire education contained the keys to dismantle and remake itself. But it would take me years to understand that.

I fell from defiance into despair. My flailing led to the pursuit of a false self. I tried my darndest to become a lawyer, and then a teacher. Occupational predictability beckoned.

Underneath the pretense and fear, I burned to be a writer, and follow that rabbit hole *all the way down.*

Eventually, I turned my back on achieving credentials through institutions. I thought I needed those degrees to make a difference. Nothing wrong with that dream, but it didn't scrape deep enough. Realizing those shoes didn't fit wouldn't spare me – but it was a start.

I found myself teaching at an experimental summer program for high school students. One day I went onstage, singing Megadeth's "Peace Sells" with an abandon I didn't even know I had, while pitching a "Heavy Metal – Art or Trash?" workshop. That pitch lured a collection of misfit students to the loading dock behind the school. We played each other music that powered/consoled us through our lives as freaks and outcasts.

A couple weeks later, I invited students to talk about living in an alcoholic family (courtesy my father). When I came out in front of all those students as just another lost mofo from a so-called broken home, I could feel the electricity. No more pretense, no more peacock feathers.

Lightbulb: my scars were the source of my creative power – as long as I displayed them without shame, *with no regard for what I might lose.*

I envied the other teachers for their storied accomplishments and Ivy League credentials. But they had not laid themselves bare in that way. My alienation transformed me into a beacon for kindreds.

The dysfunctional pain that blocked me from achieving what the other teachers had was suddenly in play. My audience felt a bond with me beyond what I would have known – if I hadn't exposed my scars through performance.

No coincidence – I met one of the greatest loves of my life through those jugular moments. I was terrified on that stage, but I was up there, dammit, and that's how I found them. Or how they found me. That connection was only made by pushing through the terror of exposure. Suddenly I had the kind of love that had always eluded me. It made a lie of all those years of gutless silence, and the blasphemy of fitting in.

I didn't make a wooden nickel from those performances. *But it changed everything.* I bet it will for you too.

No, I didn't get a huge crowd at any of those talks, but I got enough. Those who showed were attracted to a more authentic version of myself. That sparks potent friendships. It validates your push to the edge.

One week later, another talent show. In the prior show, I did a cheesy, Chippendale-style routine with some other male counselors.

I still remember the awkwardness, feeling phony and idiotic swaying my hips onstage. The cheers felt misplaced, undeserved. The night before the final talent show, I scribbled a poem in a frenzy. It was not the first poem I had written. But it was the first I would ever perform. It shimmered with all the rage and loneliness I had ever swallowed, regurgitated into something else.

I came off stage, only to get a monster hug from someone I had a huge crush on, but didn't even know that well – they seemed to understand I wasn't some kind of rock star, but someone who had struggled too many years to get up there and do that.

Being passionately embraced for the bravery of naked expression – well, it changed me. And it will change you too. It will cast a new light on adversity, and all those who still stand in your way. *Your flame burns hotter than that.*

As Ossie Davis said about jazz saxophonist Charlie Parker in Ken Burns' *Jazz* documentary:

> *"Charlie Parker, to me, was a golden cleaver that could cut the bone and release forces that we didn't know were there. He would ride the horses of extreme danger, even if they pulled them apart. And his anguish as a man and as a Black man was all folded into his relationship to the saxophone."*

When you shine, not everyone will be happier for it. Some friends were distant afterward (looking back, they should be classified as "buddies" at best). The handful who embraced my strange emergence were enough.

But it's something you've gotta think about. You've now broken the collective pact to dull it down, so we can all get on with the process of getting by, *without grappling with our profound accountability*, without wondering if there is something we can do to flip the script.

In my case, alas, that onstage recognition was also misleading. It was not an accurate reflection of the marketplace. As it turns out, people are not falling over themselves to underwrite folks who perform spoken word on napkins --> rude career awakenings ahead. Still, I tasted a strange power I had improbably – if only temporarily – claimed. It was an imprint borne of my damage, a creative risk, and yeah – a heavy dose of good fortune.

There are countless examples of artists who transfigured their scars into art – and changed the world in the process. I'm humbled by the example of James Baldwin, whose words sear off the page, a clarity fused from unfathomable pain. If you want to hear what I'm talking about, check out the audiobook version of Baldwin's *Go Tell It on The Mountain*, performed in riveting fashion by Adam Lazarre-White. I dream of having Lazarre-White record this book someday. It's not likely to happen; he's a very accomplished talent beyond my scrappy budget, but it gives me something to push for when the completion of this project seems forever beyond my grasp.

Most books on creative success seem to imagine artists building a portfolio as they triumph into art galleries, with glad-handling agents hovering. Be forewarned: this book takes you down a different path altogether. By my accounting, your dark days may not be an impediment after all. On an unreleased song, Dieselmeat's Sean Keefe sings about how he's been found out, how he's "let the secret of me out." But as he gets "beat down," a startling revelation: "No one can stop me now." Alice in Chains hits similar concepts in "Lesson Learned," referring to how, in your darkest hour, you can strike gold, and you'll know it when it happens. For our purposes here, what you lose just might conjure what you really needed.

Don't go further with this book until you have a vision for how you can emerge. Emerge as someone who is conscious of your flaws, but who can sculpt them in a way that moves others. Be ready to give up just about everything to become that sculptor. Otherwise "getting by" will rub your edges right off.

Creative Manifestation – Cultivate the Edge

Once you figure out that the scars you concealed are the why, you've got your creative edge. *Now protect that edge with your life.* You'll make decisions others find perplexing. But you will do it. Once you take the vow, there is a slow-cook exhilaration. A quiet faith in yourself will take up arms against your despair.

Fine – so what the hell do you do next? Unless a very rich relative slips on a banana peel, the world isn't going to lay down and sponsor your quirky dreams. We can't shut ourselves in a bunker for a year or two and build. If you can spare the years, go get a bunker. I call that a total immersion plan; it's good work if you can get it. Most lack the resources to unplug for such a long-term endeavor.

I hope your plan to become an artist isn't graduate school. The mad pursuit of your craft is not an academic exercise. Sure, go to grad school to acquire contacts, study your modality, or score a credential. That's not the same as becoming an artist.

I waited a long-ass time for someone to show up and fund my projects. Screw that. Crowdfunding? Gobs of supporters on Patreon? Good gigs if you can get them. Usually those crowdfunds are a few projects ahead, when folks know what you're capable of.

Be your own benefactor. Even if you're a filmmaker – arguably the most expensive creative undertaking – you'll be amazed at how much equipment you can beg or borrow (my local community television station, Northampton Open Media, loans out high caliber gear all the time; they are not alone). Hugh MacLeod, author of *Ignore Everybody*, was right: we play the "I'm saving up for gear" card as an excuse to bear down. Guess what? An advanced degree is a form of gear.

Advanced degrees are certainly not an impediment – Brian May of the legendary band Queen has a PhD, as does the ground-forging Native American folksinger Buffy Sainte-Marie. But for many, such a program would be putting off the essential self-confrontation. Artist Georgia O'Keefe is more typical of the path to artistic greatness: yes, some art school, but the big breakthroughs came after, finding new inspiration (via designer Arthur Wesley Dow), and re-inventing her craft through charcoal sketch experiments.

So yeah, be careful about school – you may just be postponing the clash your work craves. My creative life surged ahead when learn-by-doing sunk in. I'm too much of a misfit to go to grad school anyhow. I'm happier with the grittier process of creating my own credentials.

Yeah, you probably need an undergrad degree to keep the world somewhat off your neck, but even there, trade school degrees could be fine. They might be better than liberal arts degrees – if they lead to a stable occupation to fund your art. Beware of settling only for a high school diploma, unless you have a Steve Jobs "in the garage" opportunity you must pursue immediately.

If not, you're done with school and you are ready. Or, as poet Bonafide Rojas exhorts, "Make beautiful art from stark reality."

Master What You're Good At, Not What You Want to Be Good At

You only need a few things: the basic equipment to make your art, and a space to do it in (a cafe or a dingy basement qualifies). Don't be afraid of dank garages and dark corners. Or the fluorescent opposite – I started this book in the glaring chaos of a 24-hour McDonald's. I really needed that surreal kick in the ass.

You require a realistic assessment of your talent. Through trial and error, you'll figure out which mediums you excel at. Those are the ones to master. *You better love it too* – though it can be a volatile kind of love. I still struggle to write; wrestling ideas onto page is not simple for me. But I have inherent writing ability to draw on – not so when I stumble on the guitar.

You don't necessarily have to pick the thing you are most talented at, but narrowing your focus is a must. There are great lead vocalists in rock and roll who started out tentatively (e.g., James Hetfield of Metallica), or who got thrust into the role when the former lead vocalist quit (e.g., Phil Collins of Genesis).

I took visual art classes for four years in high school. I had the humiliation to paint alongside visual geniuses. I got better, but I really had to slog. Meantime, my gifted peers won accolades almost effortlessly, advancing miles for each of my bumbling steps.

After twenty years of guitar lessons (thanks Jim Armenti!), I'm just an adequate guitar player, much to my chagrin and torment. But with writing, even in high school, I somehow wrote some stuff that sparked, though I knew f-all what to do about it. I was raw as heck.

Between those three pursuits, the contrast in natural talent was striking – and a horse pill to swallow.

Fuse passion and talent. The odds are steep enough. Doesn't mean you stop the other things. I still love to fumble on my guitar – nothing beats an Alice in Chains "Nutshell" jam for me. It just doesn't qualify for the conversation we are having now.

I wrote my first spoken word poem after I somehow walked away from that hit-and-run car accident. It didn't feel like I was creating a poem from scratch. It was more like channeling something I was tuning into – like a radio station only I could find. The words were mine – and yet they weren't just mine.

Bob Dylan used similar words to express how he wrote some of his early epics. (He once claimed he wrote "Blowin' in the Wind" in about ten minutes.) Dylan also later admitted his own awe when he wrote staggering songs like "It's Alright Ma, I'm Only Bleeding."

"I don't think I could sit down now and write 'It's Alright, Ma' again. I wouldn't even know where to begin, but I can still sing it," Dylan is quoted as saying in the book *Revolution in the Air* (2009). In 1997, Dylan told the *New York Times*, "I've written some songs that I look at, and they just give me a sense of awe. Stuff like, 'It's Alright, Ma,' just the alliteration in that blows me away."

Aging doesn't always guarantee artistic greatness. Wrap your head around Prince, recording his masterpiece "Purple Rain" when he was only 26. And that was his sixth album.

That's the creative conundrum. Even with our most unabashed effort, we might not tune that frequency as strongly from one project to the next. Fortunately, the joy/burden of the artistic life persists.

Losing yourself in that creative channeling is a subtle form of ecstasy, the opposite of walking around in anxious torment. When your art tunes into that cosmic radio – even occasionally – that's a very good sign you've chosen a pursuit where you might stand out. Because you'll be graced with performances beyond what you thought possible. If that's too mystical for you, don't sweat it. But if/when it happens, you'll know.

The catch? You need enough essential skill to translate what you are tuning into (I hear melodies in my head that my klutzy guitar fingers can't play).

It's unlikely you will randomly crank something out that will change your circumstance, like the teenage SE Hinton writing *The Outsiders*, or Harper Lee publishing her very first novel, *To Kill a Mockingbird.*

The rest of us will need the discipline of time, focus, and experience. The stakes of that decision are high. Time, well – it starts flying at a disconcerting rate.

Once you pick the right creative focus, it all comes down to claiming time. Translation: you need a routine. That may be the hardest part, especially at the get-go. Your life may feel too overwhelming/ridiculous to establish any sort of creative rhythm.

Sure, you can go to writing classes or conferences. If you have work to share and contacts to make, those things can be useful. Same thing if you are genuinely stuck. It still comes back to the diligence of the solitude craft.

There's one wee problem. This deceptively simple thing – toiling away – ain't that simple. Claiming your art invokes complications. Your relationships may be thrown into question.

Routine Destroys "Someday"

"Someday" is your enemy. For me, "someday" used to mean, "Someday I will have the money/ time to write." I never found those circumstances. I waited years to have a few weeks off at the holidays to shut things down and write. It never panned out.

With each passing year, my self-loathing increased. Turns out cramming in a few weeks of massive productivity isn't so easy. Obligations and setbacks have a way of storming in. I boiled.

When you don't create, there are consequences. Your internal perfectionist gains strength. When you don't feed your work, you feed the beast of self-doubt.

You won't get anywhere without a routine. You'll end up just like I did, napkin scribbles jammed in drawers of wishful thinking, notes lost on dead computers. Or: half-baked blog sites – the ghost towns of the Internet.

Routine forces a rhythm where we are creating, learning, doing kickass stuff, doing not-so-kickass stuff, rethinking, and right back at it. As we put each iteration out there, we're taking the pulse of our audience, whether it's blog comments, open mike nights, or gallery submissions. We've invoked the practical magic of the feedback loop. Then it's down to the lab for another experiment, informed by our skirmishes.

If we persist with that rhythm, we have a real shot. The foolhardy alternative: shoot off our big ideas like roman candles, hoping to set the world on fire. Overnight success is a pipe dream. It's poison to your artistic brain.

If you're enjoying fabulous overnight success, what are you doing reading this? Toss this book in the junk pile. Come back only if you need to – hopefully never.

When you peel it back, most so-called "overnight successes" were a brutal scrape, a painstaking step-by-step – much of which happened in obscurity. I just heard Radiohead talk about that during their Rock & Roll Hall of Fame induction.

In *Outliers*, Malcolm Gladwell calculated it takes 10,000 hours to master something. I'm no Gladwell fanboy, but that sounds about right. Translation: get your tuchus in gear.

The swell thing about routines: you no longer have to sweat one hardcore deadline, or grieve your inevitable thuds. You'll post writing that few people notice, songs only your friends listen to. But you'll get your gut check anyhow.

Routines do not have to be a treadmill drag. I use "routine" in the loose sense of implied consistency: aspire to notch a creative push several times a week.

Sometimes you'll lose a week – for me, it's when I'm traveling. Cut yourself a break then. Assess your project in four week intervals. Every month, you should log at least four or five creative bursts. No excuses (yep, that includes babies, birthdays, and *most* illnesses).

If you don't get those sessions in, this book will fail you. Worse: you'll fail yourself. If you're like me, you'll start resenting the bleep out of those artists who are living their dreams.

We're avoiding our own reflection. As the years go by, the price of escaping that mirror goes up. You won't be able to cope without addictive distractions. You'll be another blown-out candle, a vigil wasted.

Trust me; you don't EVER want to feel those things. Create as you go – you'll get your share of heartbreak anyhow, without descending to the depths of creative passivity. Don't fall back on the wannabe bullpucky of "Someday I will join an artist's colony," or "When I finally get my teaching degree, I'll have summers off to write."

There's nothing wrong with a creative plan that includes periods of extended immersion – *as long as you also weave creative time into your day-to-day.*

Routine means consistently protecting your time. This has ginormous implications for emotional self-discipline, and your ability to set proper boundaries. You'll find out if those you love support these dreams – or whether they actively resist, and become part of what you are fighting.

If claiming time is a serious issue for you, I have a whole section on stealing time in *FFCA*. It's all about the practicalities of getting life-changing projects off the ground.

Once you establish a long-haul routine, you'll uncover a quiet optimism. As long as you are gifted with enough time on this crapshoot planet to follow through, you *will* get your creative work out the door. You *will* fulfill your legacy, which is really, when you boil it down, a promise to yourself.

Keep your work sessions as modest as you can. Avoid the all-night binge; find a rhythm that doesn't kibosh you.

I've got my writing sessions down to 60 minutes max. Lately, it's more like 30 minutes, on a small, cheap Chromebook that sits charged by the door, dedicated for the cause. And yeah, I have a specific bag for it too – a man purse if you must know. I can grab a work session quickly. (Update: now it's a lightweight Dell XPS and a waterproof backpack made out of truck canvas from the bag design geniuses at M-24, but the gist is the same; I'm ready. And I can get something creative done in as little as 15 minutes). Usually, I write about half nonfiction and half fiction in the same short session.

I finally got it through my (especially) thick skull: it's not how long I write, but how consistently I claim it. You want your creative sessions to give you an internal stir, but not to drain you.

If you sneak this in just a few times a week, week over week, year over year, it WILL change your life. Eventually, you may be able to double down on your time. But at first, that's all you need.

Yes, I am asking a lot of you. Our lives are already over-stuffed. I can only tell you it is worth it. Finagling writing into my startup life has required gut-check determination. *But I'm back.* That means I'm still in the game. That means I'm not squandering my life in a sea of tasks and obligations. I'll go down swinging – or typing in my case.

More than ten years ago, a friend from high school died – one of the most gifted musicians I ever knew. Neal Hutto had a hard way with himself, but such an easy way with others. My God, when he was on, he was the sun. Give Neal a piano, or a guitar, or just about any instrument, and he could make it sing. I think of Neal sometimes when I write. He'd be so disappointed in me if I capitulated. I'll bet you have a Neal in your life. Let them stoke your fires.

Your day job may bring its rewards. But only the truly fortunate will find creative freedom with a hefty paycheck. The brave, unsparing work is what you alone can discover – on your own time. When you dig for it, you'll feel that bittersweet connection to those who believed in you, even if they are physically gone.

Unplug or All Is Lost – Filter, or Fail

I see people glued to their phones all the freakin' time. If I take a nosey peek, they are usually doing something irrelevant or compulsive on Instagram or Facebook.

When I see someone with a status update addiction, a cruel thought flashes: "They will never be a great artist."

Unfair? Probably. But I know this: unplug or all is lost. Routine means nothing if you can't phase out the world, and get shit that matters out the door.

Yes, the information barrage is getting worse – but that's a sorry excuse for our underwhelming creative output. We are careless about creating filters that control the noise. If you don't get a handle on the filter problem, you will not create. You'll be sucked into the void of being known for your clever/charming social persona – and not for the bracing work that should define you.

I wouldn't impose my filtering and prioritization system on anyone. I doubt it would work, and I doubt it would fit. But maybe you can riff on it somehow:

- Step away from the all-or-nothing creative immersion time fantasy.
- Instead, create electronic "tiers of availability." Some people need to reach you all the time, day or night (boyfriends, Moms). Others (such as fussy clients) need an email response from you the same day. Others don't. Make sure all know how to reach you, on what channels, and what the limits are.
- Related, reduce your 24/7 availability. My clients and business partners know I respond to emails the same day. They also know I'm not on email all the time. If they need me ASAP, they know to send me a Twitter or Slack message.

I have a separate email address for things like weather, travel, and calendar alerts. That's the only email I get on my phone all the time. I'll add a client to that address if we are on deadline, but I avoid pings from randoms when I'm in "high filter" mode.

Writing this book is my most protected time. I write off hours when I won't be needed, mostly weekends and holidays. Yes, I have my phone with me, but the only way I can be interrupted is if someone calls me. Happily, calling has become unfashionable, so it's rare to get an intruding phone call. I usually let calls go to voicemail, and check the message transcription. Sometimes I shut that down too. "Airplane mode" is a beautiful thing – and not just when you're flying.

On my Chromebook, I typically write offline. If I am online, the only site I open is my Twitter replies. Twitter is a medium where being responsive means a lot. But if I get a bunch of replies, I'll close that out too. I almost never check emails when I am writing.

During the height of my workday, I open up my availability to "max" – that means all my email accounts are online. I'm checking LinkedIn. I have a love/hate thing with Facebook that usually veers towards hate, but I'll go on there if I get an alert from a friend, or need to approve posts for a local group. After the height of the workday, I lower my availability channels again. Many extoll the virtues of the "tech detox." But detoxing doesn't solve your ongoing smartphone distraction problem – filtering does.

Filtering systems take work to set up. Setting the right filters/priority levels is trial and error, but they give you some control back. Yes, we all want to peek in on social drama from time to time, or FaceTime someone. Fair game – IF your creative stint is done.

I still write in cafes and restaurants, but then again, I'm pretty good at keeping conversations brief. For me, writing out and about is a good thing – I actually find less distractions away from my Batcave, where a zillion projects lurk. Find your own mix. Just know: a creative routine is not enough. You also need an unplugging and filtering system.

Become a fierce protector of your own solitude. No one is going to do it on your behalf. If you protect your solitude – without falling into the quagmire of despairing loneliness – then I like your chances. Claim that time, and it will change you forever. Let it slip, and say hello to the curse of lost possibilities.

When you set up solitude boundaries and filter control, you'll upset some of your peeps. You may even mess up who you keep at a distance – and who you let in. Adjust filters accordingly. Along the way, you'll miss some last-minute potluck invites that get caught in a filter. Fine tune, and you'll get it right.

Protecting your time may seem bloody obvious – but if you're serious about your creative agenda, this is where you take your stand.

Sever the Link Between Art and Commerce

If you've tasted the toils of obscurity, it's easy to get seduced by daydreams. Someday, this comforting pipe dream goes, you'll be profusely compensated for your art.

We wishfully pine for the life of *Games of Thrones* author, George R. R. Martin – though now he has a different paymaster to contend with. As of this edit, he's permanently lost pace with the HBO show, to the detriment of both.

I've sliced and diced this till I'm delirious. It comes down to this paradox:

> *If you want a shot at creative magnificence, you must sever the ties between art and commerce first.*

You must free your art from any pressure to perform commercially. No, this doesn't apply to *all* of your creative work. If you're like me, you keep the cash flowing with paid creative work. But your art needs a project beyond marketplace demands. So does your life.

It's nice when a day job sharpens your creative axe. The more professionally stable you are, the better your chances of pushing *all* your projects along. And: a great career is a pretty darn good consolation prize.

Beyond your pro gigs, you need an unfettered creative pursuit. Your creative work needs incubation. You must protect your work in those formative stages. *You must have the material ability to walk away from proposals that would dilute your work.* But there's an unexpected twist, a most beautiful paradox. When you sever a special project from commerce, you actually enhance its potential to change lives.

One classic example comes via the Showtime documentary of Richard Pryor, *Omit the Logic.* After years of working the stand-up scene, Pryor got the break comics of his time pushed for: a full-time gig in Las Vegas. But for Pryor, the gig others pined for was a half nelson. Quoting from the documentary:

> *"He plays Vegas in 1966, and he's a huge success. And that world that he so aspired to join, wanted to impress everybody, wanted to be a big star with his name in lights – and slam, there's a hollowness to the prize."*
>
> *"When he was in Las Vegas performing, he looked out in the audience… Dean Martin was in the audience, and he was looking at him. And Richard said, 'I looked at Dean Martin through his own eyes and saw me looking like a damn fool.'*
>
> *"It was like an epiphany. 'I don't want to do it that way anymore. I want to do it the way I hear it.'*

> *That was probably when Richard Pryor decided to become Richard Pryor."*

Pryor managed to get himself fired from the so-called dream gig. Then he cranked the volume up, became a legendary stand-up performer, and an unlikely voice in the civil rights movement. A different kind of fame ensued. Did Pryor's problems magically go away? Hardly. Artists tend to be haunted or driven; fame brings new predicaments. But the lesson stands.

Creative bravery is about making the most of circumstance, however tragic. There is still the yearning; there is still the commitment to craft. Even as you read this book, your creative odds may seem insurmountable. That has certainly been the case for me lately. But there is always a story out there to jolt my pretensions: the battle against circumstance is almost universal. I have so much to learn about creative courage. While revising in December 2020, I came across this Wikipedia note on *The Diary of Anne Frank*:

> *"In June 1999,* Time *magazine published a special edition titled 'Time 100: The Most Important People of the Century.' Anne Frank was selected as one of the 'Heroes & Icons,' and the writer, Roger Rosenblatt, described her legacy with the comment, 'The passions the book ignites suggest that everyone owns Anne Frank, that she has risen above the Holocaust, Judaism, girlhood and even goodness and become a totemic figure of the modern world – the moral individual mind beset by the machinery of destruction, insisting on the right to live*

and question and hope for the future of human beings.' He notes that while her courage and pragmatism are admired, her ability to analyse herself and the quality of her writing are the key components of her appeal. He writes, 'The reason for her immortality was basically literary. She was an extraordinarily good writer, for any age, and the quality of her work seemed a direct result of a ruthlessly honest disposition.'"

And thus we are humbled – but we can also draw a spark from artistic bravery. *The power of creative work not dictated by commerce is palpable.* For me, the parallels come from music – The Doors, Nirvana, Tool, Janis Joplin, Bob Marley, Loretta Lynn, Jimi Hendrix, Billie Holiday. These folks were/are playing for keeps. That "all in" vibe gives their work a primal draw. Add Alice in Chains, Amy Winehouse, and Tupac to that list.

Yes, a lot of those musicians died young, but not all. Musical urgency is usually informed by real-life struggle, but those struggles don't have to take you under. I hear that same urgency in everyone from Chuck D to Eminem to Aretha. Johnny Cash sure had it – Neil Young still does. I hear it in Amy Lee of Evanescence, and I certainly hear it in Michael Monroe, the former lead singer of Hanoi Rocks, and someone who can still take over a stage after the age of 60.

You can cite examples from everywhere. Camus and Sartre have this power in their philosophy – their quest for truth with the threat of fascism at the doorstep, their struggles with their own contradictions

– and with each other. James Baldwin has that in so much of his writing; *Notes of a Native Son* burns from the kindling of self-confrontation, and contempt for comforting falsehoods.

The Wire is a classic TV example from HBO. Creator David Simon was determined to tell the story of American urban deterioration, but on his own terms. NBC gave him grief about the "pessimistic" tone of his prior NBC show, *Homicide: Life on the Street.* Simon took *The Wire* to HBO, where he'd be free to do his unsparing portrayal of urban Baltimore, without network TV buzzards circling.

The result? Some of the best television you'll ever see. *The Wire* got mediocre ratings and little fanfare when it came out. Now it has a cult fan base, and critical adoration as one of the greatest TV shows ever made. Yet it will never match the commercial heft of *Game of Thrones* or *The Walking Dead.* If David Simon was about getting paid, a CSI-style crime syrup variation would have been the lazier/easier bet.

Look, there's plenty of room for commercially-savvy art, like the disposable candy of a perfect pop song (Michael Jackson's masterful "Billy Jean" comes to mind, or if you're down on Michael Jackson these days, maybe "Larger than Life" by the Backstreet Boys, "Little Red Corvette" by Prince, or "I Gotta Feeling" by The Black Eyed Peas). But as the encroachment of commercialism hits every aspect of our lives, the appetite for defiant art grows.

Sometimes, you can do both. Seeker's "Remedy" is a classic example; a ridiculously catchy song about a grim battle with drug addiction. I think of the aforementioned Dave Houghton's prior band, The Reejers. If you're lucky, on YouTube you can catch their classic "Coffee Grounds," which has that 90s poppy/grungy vibe, until out of nowhere, Houghton howls something about being born scarred, and born on trial. To this day, it cuts through me. Bold and poppy don't have to contradict.

With that in mind, you might choose to sell your work. You might even sell the rights to one project to fund others. Another way to go: take an equity or profit-sharing stake on an independent project, in lieu of salary. It can lead to a nice payoff – if you can cope without the paid gig, or fund it on the side. At Readercon 2019, I talked with a successful novelist who is also a ghost writer for hire. Just make sure you have a skilled copyright lawyer on your side, so you know exactly what you're signing away.

By all means, create work for money – *especially if it advances your relevant skills.* The word "relevant" is critical here – I remain haunted by my college friend Joe Minton's prophetic warning: "I'm afraid of becoming mediocre by excelling at useless things." Farm a creative garden plot of your own, plant whatever you damn well please – and see what sprouts.

You are the true arbiter of your own excellence. To this day, some of my obscure work is my best. The audience was anything but huge, but the depth of those who did respond affirmed the direction.

The power of free dovetails with axing the commercial agenda. Free your digital work to attract an audience. As you build that audience, ways to monetize expand. Always keep the principle of funding your own work as an option; audiences come with expectations of their own. You must be free to re-invent, to put out work that might roil your existing "fans."

Music history is marked by artists who had to turn their backs on fans to get where they needed to go. Or, more accurately, they turned their backs on their fans' rabid expectations for more of the same. Arguably the most infamous example in music history: a defiant Bob Dylan plugged in his electric guitar on Saturday, July 24, 1965, at the Newport Folk Festival. According to Jonathan Taplin, a roadie working at Newport, Dylan made a sudden decision to challenge the festival by performing with a fully amplified band the following evening.

As Taplin recounts it, Dylan's view was "'Well, fuck them if they think they can keep electricity out of here, I'll do it. ' On a whim, he said he wanted to play electric." So Dylan assembled a band and got it done, amidst a chaotic mix of cheers and boos. One writer, believed to be John Gilliland, said Dylan "electrified one half of his audience, and electrocuted the other."

That's a big reason why crowdfunding has limitations. It's also why I worry about fan-funded art being idealized as the way forward. People usually want more of what they got a taste of. You, however, might need to move on to other experiments. And you should. Otherwise your molting for re-invention will wither into handing out pudding cups, when you know deep down, you should be moving on, just as everyone from Lou Reed to Miles Davis to Aretha Franklin did before you.

Brave work will alienate some, even while it changes others. It helps enormously when you don't have to pay the rent from those adventures.

Popular Success Is Unlikely – and Irrelevant

This book used to have a chapter called "Success is an Algorithm." I've pulled it for self-indulgence, though I may post it online. I broke down popular success into an algorithm, where all the factors, from genetic beauty to inherited wealth, from natural-born talent to health problems, were all laid out.

I wanted to prove the misguided utopia called "commercial success" is beyond our control – albeit with factors we can absolutely influence.

Sometimes, our persistence in the face of daunting odds is what makes our struggle beautiful. Other times, there is a brutal/whimsical randomness. Look at a film like *Searching for Sugarman*, which documents how early '70s musician Rodriguez was famous in South Africa but had no idea, for most of his life, of that important fact.

If popular success is fickle, commercial success for distinctive art is even more improbable.

The Strange Redemption of "Enough"

There is hope, but it comes with a plot twist. *Redemption comes from redefining the end goal.* Maybe, amidst the frenzy of consumption, addiction, and compulsive career climbing, we'll nudge into the mystical land of "enough."

For artists, enough means sufficient audience/ income to free us for the work that matters most. When you cross over into enough, your best work becomes your day job. You've found a lasting truce between art and commerce. It's an elusive achievement, but you can squander your life on worse aims.

Maybe you can use that brazen work – or the visibility coaxed from it – to destroy the wall between commerce and savage authenticity. It's worth a dice roll.

If you don't protect your fiercest work, nobody else will. They'll pay you for an airbrushed version of yourself. The years pile up as you ghost write the bland, or illustrate on spec. Getting paid is a good thing – just make sure you are funding something more potent.

Great artists can fail. By economic standards, the vast majority will. How we internalize that narrow definition of failure and fall in line is one of the big lies.

If your published work emanates your truth, there is no such thing as failure.

Disappointment? Yes. Absurdity that your work is overlooked while Tony Robbins, Michael Bolton, Nickelback, Spice Girls, and Carrot Top sell out arenas? Absolutely.

I've put out bold work with high hopes, only to have it land with a commercial thud. The high school version of me, craving a type of fame I now see as irrelevant, would have been bitterly disappointed.

Here's what I didn't expect. When I put uncompromising work into the world, I don't feel like I suck. Failure is the years where my hangups got the best of me. *I feel failure not for my artistic imperfections, but for my silence.*

Sometimes I feel a seductive, more terrifying version of failure: I get paid handsomely for diluted work. Tread carefully – that's the stuff lifestyle addictions are made of.

I think back to that high school version of myself, so full of mad ambition and dreams of massive impact. Would I be disappointed in how my life turned out? Yes and no.

The high school version of me was right about one thing: dream a big-ass dream. We should always bring the fire. But I didn't understand what I was up against. I didn't understand we are entitled to nothing. I severely underestimated the redeeming/uncanny adventures of throwing yourself into the proper journey. I put too much weight on glorious outcomes. Oh, and I also underestimated what I call the "emotional undertow" of past trauma.

The real triumph is what you overcome inside yourself. It's not the day the *New York Times* reviews your book. It's the day you hold that first copy in your hands, humbled by all you confronted to reach that once-unfathomable point.

It's a flash of gratitude: you were given the chance. *Sure, you seized it, but something met you halfway.* You were blessed with time, while others just as worthy got a cremation. And yet, you didn't brag or wallow. You used that time with all the brazen fortitude you could muster. That, my friends, is success. That is the victory over convention.

That is you, from the gravel road you were birthed on, bronzed by riddles only you could decipher, exposed by the nakedness of your best art. On that day, you should be proud indeed. If you need a herd of fans to validate that fateful moment, then something went terribly wrong.

Your Day Job Can't Suck

Artists often take the no-brainer, clock-out day job in order to preserve time for art. That's a dangerous choice.

If you're making good creative progress; if you're not falling into debt; and you're not slogging a problematic job that drains you, *then put this book away – and get on with it.*

Otherwise, let's think this through.

Be wary of low-ceiling jobs that demand too much mentally or physically. It's the "fast forward five years" problem. If you're still working that crummy job five, ten years from now, you're putting too much heat on your creative work to bail you out.

CAVEAT: If the day job allows you to save more than you can spend, that changes things. I explain how to move from savings to income-generating assets in *Free From Corporate America*, so I won't detail that here. The gist? Stashing cash gives you lifestyle flexibility down the road.

One trap I've seen herds of musicians fall for: waiting tables or bartending. These jobs can pay pretty well. They are ideal as part of a musician's lifestyle – flexible shifts and so on. You can even hit the road and score a similar job upon return. Some restaurant gigs pay well enough to stockpile cash. But as the years advance, these jobs put tread on your tires. You hit the skills and satisfaction ceiling long before that.

Back problems, sore feet, or burnt-the-hell-out – these are the risks of the service industry professions. Not to mention fast living, over-spending on drugs, and the wake-and-bake lifestyle that often comes with food service. Sales might be a tad better. You probably won't advance much, but if you're good at sales, that gives you a bunch of employment options (I mean actual sales positions where you are paid to close deals, not retail registers). Trade jobs like electric and carpentry can work well, and pay decently – as long as your body holds up.

Claim a career you find halfway tolerable, if not rewarding. Whatever funds your art with the least downside. For some, that's teaching. With the right credentials, you can do okay, especially in a two-income household. Summers off are a creative asset. For others, it's the Uber/Lyft/TaskRabbit gig economy. Awesome for flexibility, not awesome for actually making a decent wage.

Another tactic: find a career that connects to your art, and strengthens your skills/contacts. A musician becomes a studio producer; a painter becomes a gallery manager; a writer becomes a managing editor. I've seen all of the above work. It might not be as thrilling as churning out your own stuff, but it keeps you in the industry.

If you're passionate about your day job, the balance sheet of life tends to work out. Bonus: when the time comes to pitch your side project, those contacts will matter.

I've never aged more than when I busted on grueling jobs that didn't further goals. If you're like me, you'll end up hating yourself for falling into the grind. You'll feel like a sellout or a burnout, or some horror show blend of the two. Your exhaustion from the workweek is the final indignity, making it dismally hard to create.

Consider Hugh Macleod's "sex and cash theory":

"The creative person has two kinds of jobs: one is the sexy, creative kind. The second is the kind that pays the bills. Sometimes the assignment covers both cases, but not often."

Macleod brings up Hollywood actors who score big paychecks for the big screen, funding their "pro bono" in independent films, or even in theater, as my former college classmate Liev Schrieber has done (I use the term "classmate" loosely here).

Or: they roll the dice on a piece of the profit, and take nothing upfront. Either way, some projects fund others. That's the sex and cash theory.

Macleod urges us: eradicate the falsehood that certain jobs are beneath us. Self-financed subversion is an art unto itself. Anything that gets us there...

Be wary of entrepreneurial business. Yeah, I have a passion for it, but it shreds time. Forget about days – I've had months, no, make that years, when I didn't get much done artistically. Talk about an existential horse pill. If your creative imprint is building startups, that's a different story.

The startup advantage: you'll learn to become the financial caretaker – and guerrilla marketer – of your own creative endeavors.

My business invokes the learning curve of multi-media: photography, podcasts, videos. Video gave me skills I might use to land gigs when I need it most. If I want to make a film someday, or be a script supervisor, I'm somewhere on that path as well.

At its best, the "day job" of running my company pushes skills and furthers causes. And, since I'm an equity partner, maybe I'll actually own something of value down the road.

I put myself through an exacting daily question: *Is the life I have today the one I am willing to have forever?* The answer might not sooth, but it motivates.

My professional life pushes my limits in a way I crave. It puts me on airplanes and lands on adventures. And: I figured out how to squeeze in a dash of my own stuff on the side.

Not as much as I'd like. Not as much as when I fancied myself some kind of Hunter S. Thompson American madman. Dreams die hard – but some of them morph into a life that suits you. I don't regret pushing my life to the extremes, but you can't linger there.

As David Lee Roth of Van Halen drawled in one of rock's most riveting moments, "You know I've been to the edge… and there I stood and looked down." Yes, you can pull wisdom from such extremes, but as Roth warns, "You know I've lost a lot of friends there." As have we all.

I had no idea the price of the ticket. I never want to lose that burn of brazen youth, even if it's not as easy to light that blowtorch these days.

It's about a swap between sheer energy and experience. It's a swap I can live with, as long as I am still fierce. It's a shift I can live with – as long as I'm still in the game. Job one: make sure you can always say that.

I recently found myself on the Boston T, redlining a train to Cambridge, the site of grandiose dreams upon college graduation, way too many years ago.

I was wrong about almost everything back then. I was wrong about being a city mouse and an urban player. I thought proclaiming yourself an artist ushered in a life of bohemian counterculture glamour. Wrong again.

Now I know: You fight for your art. Every day. As MacLeod puts it: It will cost you your life. Not all at once, but in chunks, each time you push work out, failing, creating, flailing, succeeding, careening into recognition, paid with the coin of discipline and the hefty surcharge of lost youth.

Unfathomable as it may sound, this steep price is still a bargain. It beats the fraudulence of "getting by" every time.

Pull Gold from the Feedback Loop – and Lose the BS

How much feedback do you need, and how do you alchemize it? Yes, your work should be edgy and uncompromising – but what your audience thinks also counts.

If you're a stand-up comic, you have no choice. Fail/fail/fail and then finally – someone laughs. Paraphrasing Alec Baldwin in his notorious *Glengarry Glen Ross* "Always be closing!" scene, that's a tough racket.

I dropped out of writing in college; I couldn't stomach snotty assclowns critiquing my work. I was postponing the inevitable.

The best criticism I ever got stung like stingrays. Some of it came from people I don't respect – or even like. That didn't change the validity of their critiques. The Internet adds an unsparing immediacy. It is as invaluable as it is brutal.

One of the finest books on creativity, the aforementioned *Ignore Everybody* by Hugh MacLeod, comes close to resolving this paradox.

How do we produce commercially indifferent art while earning an audience, accounting for their expectations?

Internet popularity is fickle as hell – the opposite of a meritocracy. Yes, some brave work – like *Orange is the New Black* or *Girls* – finds enough of an audience. Others, like *The Leftovers* or *Deadwood*, barely get away with a few seasons, floated by critical acclaim and the clout of its creators.

Be your own arbiter. It took decades, but I no longer need anyone to tell me which pieces are good, which are great, and which aren't so special. Now and again, my writing soars.

Mostly, I don't soar at all. I crank out words regardless. Revising is as rewarding as it is arduous. I can polish mediocre drafts into something else entirely. This is my seventy-fifth time through this manuscript; I'm still trying to spread poetry onto ideas.

In college, I badly needed approval from professors I admired. Problem is, if you're attached to approval, you're attached to criticism.

One day, I stumbled on harsh private feedback from two professors, dishing about my work. It carved me. It changed how I thought about myself. I vowed to be better. It was years before I could absorb that feedback in a dispassionate way.

Those who assess your work do so from their own dirty windshield. Take what's useful, discard the rest.

Be gloriously indifferent in all you take in, but find a way to listen regardless.

What if your less compelling work finds a bigger audience than your finest pieces? No easy answers, but it does happen. As I've said, a narrower audience that truly absorbs your work beats a bigger audience that skims off the top. But hey, if you can build a monster audience that's ridiculously passionate, like Foo Fighters or Lady Gaga did, then you won't need me, or this book, for much longer.

And that, folks, is the closest we're gonna get to resolving the "Ignore Everybody paradox." We tap into feedback early and often. We examine the agendas of those who critique our work, and why. But in the end, it's our call.

To get sensitive souls writing, I tell them: our first draft is for ourselves; our final draft is for our audience. It's true – but only to a point. *Our work must always be blatantly monogamous to our vision of it.* No matter who it offends or fails to please.

Set the tone early in your career, a la Bob Dylan, the Beatles, and David Bowie. You'll create what you see fit; your "fans" can join you if they so choose. Otherwise you're Styx, stuck playing the conceptual "Mr. Roboto" in front of fans who wanted "Blue Collar Man." A brand can be a prison, a niche a rut. That's the essence of the ignore everybody message – at least to me.

The Artistic Perils of Friendship

If you make a bold pursuit of art, your relationships are in for a jolt. Some of us scream from the womb to our own beat. We lock ourselves in our bedroom with Hendrix, Cobain, and Jimmy Page, powerchording until our families' ears bleed. Those rare few put everyone on notice early. But to surface art later in life, you *will* disrupt those you love.

If your friends claim to support your work, how could you sour things by getting serious? Brace yourself. In college, I realized my life was too dysfunctional to support creative work. I put myself through drug treatment.

Extracting myself from the drama I previously welcomed was rough stuff – all the worse because I had no way of explaining it. The whole thing felt violent. I hadn't learned how to shed skin without betraying those around me.

Decades later, I haven't been able to put things right with some of those people. I promised quite a bit more than I delivered.

Putting my creative life in the center – and doing whatever it took to protect it – changed the rules of engagement. It was liberating on one level, and brutal on another.

New people in my life understood: I put my creative life at the core. My strange disposition made more sense. No, it didn't make me a picnic to deal with – but at least they knew what they were getting into. It might seem harsh; it might seem selfish. But if you're serious about your craft, protecting that spark is job one.

Once I got a better handle on my own absurdity, I was able to articulate my odd path to those around me in a half-coherent way. Then, and only then, the people in my life could make informed decisions on my toxicity levels, and whether my particular brand of intimacy was worth the trouble.

People who truly have your back are rare. People who yearn to see you shine are rarer still (those types aren't usually the same, by the way). That's ok. You're entering a time in your life where, aside from a few core relationships, you'll be less people-focused anyhow. People are going to fail you, just as you are going to fail them.

When you take gutty steps towards your most potent/creative self, expect resistance. Adversity is how your fate is honed. *What you lose as a consequence is precisely what gives your work its soul.* A real-life example that speaks to me: young Dave Mustaine, reeling on a New York City street corner, kicked out of the Metallica tour van, scrapes himself off the existential pavement, opts not to drink himself further into oblivion, and goes on to form Megadeth, one of the greatest thrash metal bands there ever was or will be. At one time it was just bitterness – and perhaps bitter tears. But as Mustaine later sang, he put those tears in a vial. He faced his detractors.

Sometimes that resistance will be internal, sometimes external. The slang term "haters" is derived, in a simplistic way, from this phenomenon. In case I haven't said it clearly enough:

Amongst your friends are dream killers. You must root them out, and do it with the kindest ruthlessness you can muster.

No one gets a pass. Some who are threatened by your creative emergence will be the same peeps who once had your back. Being there for you in a time of pain or loss is categorically different than rooting for triumphs that may pull you into a different world.

Try cheering someone on when they land a big creative success while you are toiling in obscurity. You may say the happy things, but inside, you're grappling with "life isn't fair" resentment. I always feel ashamed when I react like that.

Want to purge that resentment? Free yourself. No, you can't free yourself all at once, but you can do it in bits and pieces. Every time I fight with this manuscript, I face my own creative doubt, my own woulda/

coulda/shoulda. I don't need commercial success to solve that bitterness – just a proper self-confrontation. I put words to page; resentment dissipates, and all is well. My own skin suits me again.

Well, almost. I still taste vinegar from those I disappointed. That's something I never want to lose. I'm just as capable of betrayal as anyone else. You can't fix the brokenness of the past – but your art is the bittersweet way forward.

The Creative Virtues of Selfishness

If you are serious about creative emergence, detoxify selfishness. Protect your creative time, or this world will grind you into the sawdust of getting by.

If you are driven to create, but unable to claim that time, your relationships will be compromised.

Yes, there *is* a yucky kind of selfishness, a self-absorbed entitlement we all recoil from. Fortunately, artists are not typically encumbered by those particular blind spots, aside from an unflattering tendency towards the pretentious. Artists sense the world beyond themselves, perhaps to a fault.

Yes, artists can fall down in their personal relationships – I know I do – but usually, a lack of sensitivity is not the artist's problem.

Embrace the paradox of selfish pursuits. You can't sustain anyone else until you feed yourself. As an artist, you feed yourself through the dogged pursuit of your elusive muse. Put that in the center of your life, or drift into a false narrative.

The missteps occur when you treat your art as the only thing that matters. That's arrogant dysfunction. Bet on ruthless practicality instead. Claim a routine that puts your art first. Via that creative extraction, you'll summon the right attitude for your other commitments. Yes, a crying baby or an unmilked cow obviously comes before the pottery wheel. My message still holds.

We condemn selfishness for reasons right and wrong. The right: being a narcissistic jerk is a drag on society. The wrong: we are unnerved by those who break away from the tribe.

When you move out of your tribe and into your art, expect to be viewed as selfish. It will not be understood. It's not easy to tune out the myopia of peer pressure, but it helps to grasp the primal reasons for it. We are tribal at our evolutionary core.

"Pay yourself first" is an investment strategy. Financial advisors warn us: if you don't take your paycheck and invest part of it off the top, when it comes to the end of the month, you won't have any money left to invest. It will disappear in Amazon Prime, or Justin Timberlake's acoustic tour.

There is logic to "pay yourself first" – though maybe we should call it "paint yourself first" for our purposes here.

I don't know if you're religious or not. Doesn't matter. Paint yourself first is still a profound act of faith. It's a vow of no-capitulation to hectic circumstances.

It takes a long-ass time for the mortgage payments of creative work to add up. But the act of doing so changes us. Granted, not right away. Once it becomes habit, the magic sets in. It's subtle magic at first – reluctant even. Pay those dues with stubborn consistency. One day, that magic will creep up and smack you.

The Strange Logic of "Paint Yourself First"

"Paint yourself first" is intended to play out over a month or so. In the day-to-day, glaring problems might take priority. But don't let a month go by without working that canvas. Find your rhythm.

I have about 1,000 work sessions logged on this book. That's how I'll rip this one out – in short bursts over years. The draft is on Google Drive; I can grab it on any browser.

Claiming time amidst adversity is changing me. Yeah, some weeks kick my ass. But I now have a creative workflow for all times – even when I'm sleep-deprived and gutting deadlines.

And – for the first time ever – I am not grinding myself down. You can't afford to blow yourself out chasing projects with a distant commercial payoff. You're playing the long game now. Pull an hour, not an all-nighter. Take it from me – you don't want to be an art zombie.

It's going be the hardest thing you've ever done. But you will do it. And someday, you'll send me the results. That will be a great day for you, and an even better one for me. Because I still question the why of it from time to time, and so will you. But – we press on. If this chaos-tested creative system didn't work, I'm not sure that I could.

Art Contre Love – Relationships Can Lift You, or They Can Sink You

Given my stance on selfishness, you may think I will now condemn relationships as a distraction from your all-important art. I take the opposite position – almost.

Life is way too grueling to deny yourself companionship from someone who is singular about you. Especially if they push you to unearth your best. But there's a big ol' catch: this type of rare jewel expects something equally singular in return, rather than dirty paint brushes and scribble poems on paper scraps.

Contrary to the stereotype of the selfless spouse, the right person for you will have a similar commitment to their own creative life. They'll cultivate their own garden when you are toiling – rather than partying without you.

Note, however, this does *not* mean that they should be as driven as you. Ideally, they will have a more "laid back" demeanor.

Two equally driven people aren't usually compatible in the long run. If they are driven by different things, maybe. But it helps if one of the two has a nesting instinct, and is able to keep the homestead humming.

There must be trust in the time apart. Your partner should look forward to solitude – or family time away from you – just as much as you look forward to your creative fix.

There *is* one type of person who will *not* work as an artists' companion. Yup – that's the "*couples do everything together*" type. I've seen that fall apart many a time. When your creative fuel is solitude, there's no way to please someone like that.

I don't believe a single artist can sustain the momentum of an artist in a forward-thinking relationship. There's just too much benefit in someone who believes in you. Especially if they fill in the practical things you overlook – assuming they find such tradeoffs acceptable.

HOWEVER, when you are faced with a relationship that is emotionally compromised or disrespectful, versus going it alone, *you go it alone* – even if that person *does* help in practical/financial terms. And yes, that includes living in the dysfunctional family basement while your self-esteem drains. Move the F out.

If you're emotionally compromised, it will infect your art.

Going it alone is, at best, bittersweet. But flying solo gifts you a high bar by which your relationships can – and should – be judged. You accept the mystery of the unrequited. No, you channel it. You infuse your art with whatever you've lost, or have yet to experience. Don't let someone put a ring on your finger until you feel the harmony between that ring and your creative drive.

Just remember, healthy relationships can be subtle, quite unlike the dysfunctional chemical romances artists like you and me tend to idealize, Bonnie-and-Clyde or Sid-and-Nancy style.

If you ever find that gold-hearted ninja that feeds your soul, don't bestow upon them the artist's notorious habit of personal neglect. Communicate how you will protect your creative time – *and* honor theirs. It's the absence of such talk that foils these things.

Give as good as you get, or you'll find your partner-in-crime in the rearview. The true keepers are hard to replace. Give them your best, do your damndest to spare them your worst, and don't let them go.

Sacrifice over Gratification – The Art of Saying "No"

We've been misled by modern fantasies that "you can have it all." Toss in: "If you dream it, you can do it!" It's a damaging way to understand success – or happiness, for that matter. It's even more misleading for the artist.

Sacrifice is a daily practice. The artist must learn to say no, and say no often. Turn down wedding invites, pare down leisure time, blow off aimless trips to the mall, no thanks to Netflix, chill, smoke a bowl, and so on.

A shred of good news: there *is* such a thing as "correct sacrifice," an idea I got from Pat Benatar. Correct sacrifice is the mystical phenomenon that if you give up the right things, it won't feel like a sacrifice in the final accounting.

It will feel more like the best (and only) choice in a predicament uniquely yours. Only you can judge what you need to give up. Yes, you'll feel the sting of opportunities missed. That's a damn sight better than losing your creative spark. Think of sacrifice as the cost of ensuring your existential outcome. That will make uttering the word "no" easier.

This is *not* about giving up primal needs for intimacy and sustenance. It *is* about peeling life to its essence: to a core of creative mastery, a viable trade, health upkeep, and not much else. It's about protecting the essential at the cost of that which is not. Walk the dog, feed the chickens, and let the rest go. To hell with gadget culture and the accumulation of miscellany. Laughter in the face of the absurd – well, you might want to keep that.

Aggressive simplicity is usually enough to power your creative output. Unfortunately, the success algorithm has variables beyond control that work against you, such as pricey medical mishaps. In those cases, you'll need to dig even deeper. And guess what? There *is* more you can do, another card you can play. Yep – that's why you're reading *The Book of Last Resort.*

Giving (Hypothetical) Blood – A Last Resort

What if success eludes you? What if your creative work is festering? If nothing else solves your existential riddle, there is more. Two responses are straightforward – and one is wrenching.

First, live leaner. Refine your expenses, especially the monthly costs. Make that a daily discipline – until you no longer feel an intense conflict between your financial life and your art.

I have a friend who did his spoken word thing for years, while holed up in a decidedly non-luxurious Bronx neighborhood. The last apartment he lived in was finally condemned. You might not be willing to go that lean. But once you start paring down, it may start to appeal – see the "tiny house movement" for more on that. (*Free From Corporate America* gets into the problem of lifestyle profitability in depth).

Once you have month-to-month financial viability, you can let up on this discipline a little, but only a little. If you relax into surplus, that surplus will dissipate.

The best use of excess cash is *not* the typical lifestyle bump, or better vacations. It's not even the stock market or 401ks. It's investing in creative ventures and skills development.

The next tactic is: change your world view – and your timeframe. This is your life, not a pharmaceutical-driven push to "make it big." You may not get there in three months – doesn't matter. Could be five years, could be ten.

It's the life you chose, or that chose you, or somewhere in between. Once that sinks in, things change. You are dedicating your entire life to this. Now you won't feel as much pressure for the short term. You won't agonize over a breakthrough that is eluding you.

You've invoked an epic and uncertain adventure. *If you're granted enough time on this ludicrous rock, you'll get the work done.* If you run out of time, you'll have bigger problems – or no more problems, depending on how you look at it. Your priorities are set. Now, you pace yourself.

Alas, there are times when those two approaches fall short. Then – and only then – you'll need something more extreme. I call this "giving blood." That's unfair to those who give actual blood regularly; that's a good idea also, but anyhow...

Giving (hypothetical) blood is your secret weapon, but you never want to use it – unless your back is up against the proverbial wall. What is giving blood? Well, it's more than giving your life over to art. It's more than making tough choices about your time, or making the so-called "right sacrifice." Giving blood cuts deeper:

It's about giving something up in the present you never thought you could live without.

You can tell when you are giving blood. It means giving up something that really hurts to live without. It might be a concert it breaks you to miss. It might be important friends you don't have time for. It might be more than that:

It might be almost everything you have.

I don't recommend this path, but I've been down it. I've tasted its reckless power. Sometimes it's the only way to get work out the door.

Giving blood is not sustainable. The price is Everest-high, including profound bouts of loneliness that are beastly to get through – or walk back from later.

But it is better than losing yourself. It is better than losing your work. It is better than giving up. The only thing that's off limits when you give blood: your health. You must never compromise that.

One extreme example: you could decide you only have time for your health, your work, and your art. That means friendships on the fly only, community where you can stumble upon it, but no significant relationships outside of family, and maybe not even that. Not necessarily celibate, though that is another choice.

Basically, you withdraw. Pull your commitments to the bone.

This stuff is no joke. But it's a card you can play when you'd rather die than be stuck where you are. If success is an algorithm, this is another variable you can influence, and change your mathematical prospects. It's truly a last resort tactic, potent but devastating.

You may not even realize the cost, until that inevitable evening where your art isn't enough – and you're completely alone. When that happens, step back, get a good night's sleep, get a hug and a nice meal and figure out what's next. Hopefully, you'll have some terrific art to show for it.

Giving blood is a just-break-glass technique. I hope you never need it. Use it *only* if the alternatives are as bleak as a heroin needle.

Do not sacrifice more quality of life than you absolutely have to. But if you burn for greatness, and your life is affording you no shot, you may be shocked by the power of this method. I've used it to transform my career while keeping the words flowing. I would not be in a creative trade today if I didn't apply these tactics to transform my circumstance. But what I had to give up stunned me. Some of those things never came back. That too I have to live with.

What I can tell you is that even on the bad days, I still feel that spark. Sometimes it's down to a flicker, but I've never let it go out. Anything to keep the creative death of existential compromise out of my heart had to be done. Whatever was lost – that was the price.

As you give blood, *you'll be saying no a lot*, protecting the slivers of time you have left. You'll also be creative as heck, melting art into the margins of your life: in the doctor's waiting room, in the afternoon when your kids are finally napping.

I've written when I'm sick – though I'm careful about that one now. I've written when I have absolutely no hope at all. I've written at that 24-hour McDonald's countless times, rubbing shoulders with stoned hipsters, drunk frat boys, and miscellaneous night wanderers.

Giving blood comes down to "whatever it takes."

How bad do you want it?

Life tests us precisely to find that out.

Giving blood is NOT about a crazy push to the physical limits. Pushing to exhaustion is a deadly approach that punishes those you care about while landing you in a hospital bed (yep, done that too). Your physical limits are verifiable. Treat that edge with respect.

Giving blood is about developing a lean rhythm, "stealing time" wherever you can. Yeah, that means missing out on drastically important things. I've missed funerals, weddings. I've let friendships fade on my watch. I've missed once-in-a-lifetime shows. Things you can't brush off afterwards.

But you'll be amazed by how much your work blossoms in these protected timeframes, when you're not stretched too thin by obligation. Just don't do it for long. Be clear to those who still love you: you don't intend to make this a lifestyle.

Yes, you will lose friends who don't understand your brute force resolve and loner tendencies.

But others *will* understand – if you let them in. You owe it to them to explain this drastic course of action. After all, you're not trying to hurt them. *All you want to do is save your goddamn soul.*

The payoff is real… IF, and only if, you can stay the course. But be warned: this won't feel like "right sacrifice." It will feel more humbling, like you are losing things that matter. And you are.

If you live this way for years on end, you'll be confronted by an emotional pileup.

Jumpstart Your Art – and Save Yourself

That's why giving blood is a jump-start technique, not a way of life. Yes, I jump-started this book with bleary late night stints at McDonald's. But once the pages piled up, I gave up that grueling schedule. I shifted to something more sustainable.

But those ridiculous McDonald's nights with Chromebook in tow sent me an internal message: *whatever it takes, baby*. Eventually, the message sunk in. Now, that 24-hour McDonald's locks doors at midnight. I'll never forget where the jump-start happened though.

It took me almost 15 years to gamble on this ruthless method. Once I did, I stopped dreaming about writing books, and started publishing them. Instead of getting caught without a career, I created one out of podcasting, and blogging into the night.

Until one day, my last-ditch dice roll got traction. I found a market for my semi-burnt offerings. So if you're truly stuck, riff on this tactic, and pull it into your life. Just don't literally do anything bloody – that was a metaphor, nothing more!

Do not allow the despair of your creative struggle and flawed circumstance turn into self-destructive actions. Before too long, you will be manifesting. And manifesting is one of the best ways out of despair.

Just know: you are not alone. Yes, perhaps in your day-to-day, you are. But not in a fundamental sense. As impossible as it may seem, the world desperately needs your voice – despite its apparent indifference.

Your Success Better Be Weird Enough

Marketing guru Seth Godin wrote a sparkling little book about success, *We Are All Weird.* Inspired by his book, I've adapted this phrase:

"Is your success weird enough?"

Godin says the digital age allows you to connect with narrow audiences around the "weird" – interests too narrow to serve via mass markets. Yet in digital markets, you can figure out how to serve niche audiences – as long as you can reach them online.

Godin proposes an economic philosophy around celebrating the "weird", and turning that into weird businesses.

I'll add this twist: *Claiming your own brand of weird makes your professional life more fulfilling – and your creative work shine.*

The "weirder" your professional livelihood is, the more uniquely suited it is to the baffling wondermuss that is you. The more your career emanates from "weird" capabilities that are uniquely yours, the more effective you will be, the more satisfying the work will be, and: the harder it will be for others to compete against you.

In my work as a tech/biz analyst and blogger, I take the question "Is your success weird enough?" as a challenge: inject as much soul into my work as possible. Instead of just paying my dues or doing what others do, I try to make the work uniquely mine. I try to bend convention with imagination and take chances. Maybe it's long-form podcasting when everyone is crying about attention spans; maybe it's taking satirical chances others don't.

And guess the F what? The more I put my stamp on the professional world in unique ways, the better it's working out. I now regret the years I treated my business generically, as a day job to fund other projects.

Not all occupations allow for "weird." Some allow way more than mine. But there are *always* ways to inject personality into what you do. At first, managers and supervisors may scratch heads. But when they see your motivation – and unwillingness to back down – they just might embrace you. If not, move on, and settle in with those that do.

Some won't grasp your brand of weird, but others will relate to your work better. Relatability matters. So whatever you do to pay the rent, make it satisfyingly "weird." To me, weird just means doing it on your own terms, like opening your own restaurant instead of flipping robotic burgers for the man.

"Is your success weird enough" dovetails nicely with the pursuit of creative power, which I sometimes call "freak power." As we've discussed, freak power is the subversive process of taking something you have a fascination with, something that might make you feel different or extreme, and manifesting it. Like Hendrix sang, you stop being ashamed of your inner freak, and wave that damn flag high.

When you do that, others are drawn to you. You might even find a tribe of sorts, one that makes you feel less alone than the hollow popularity of high school, or the cruel distribution of Instagram likes.

Freak power should generate a welcome sense of community, even if that community is geographically dispersed. *But it may not create a commercially viable pursuit.*

Example: You form a funky band that never extends beyond local gigs. Playing in an awesome local band can change your life, even if it doesn't bring you fame and fortune. It's a form of freak power. Unless you play it safe and join a cover band.

Caution: you won't be able to take full advantage of freak power in your 9 to 5. Freak power is about excavating the darkest corners, mucking about in the odd/terrifying things you find there, and alchemizing them. Then: perfecting your format until its resonates. That requires a patience and free expression beyond the scope of most employers. This is quite a few notches beyond Seth Godin's call to embrace a "weird" business niche.

However, as Godin documents, embracing the weird *can* become a viable source of income – if you nurture it along while you build an audience, or figure out a business model. But it takes time.

Monetizing true freak power is even harder. Yes, you can find examples of freak power at a commercially viable level, whether it's Björk, film director and author John Waters, or the late Kurt Vonnegut.

But when you dig into the biographies, you learn about the toil it took to turn the "weird" into something with financial weight. Not to mention the fortuitous. Jack Kerouac and his beat generation comrades didn't go on the road to get famous. They were headed to the edge; a mass audience was just another strange byproduct. And: you might not find the mass audience. At different points in rock history, musicians such as the Velvet Underground, MC5, Iggy Pop, Pixies, Patty Smyth, Hanoi Rocks, and Sonic Youth harnessed that freak power energy, and earned underground credibility. They didn't have the commercial heft of some peers – but the greats know exactly who they are.

On the other hand, The Doors rode that freak power energy to the top of the charts, leaving us with singular creations like "The End," which I believe best captures the subversive power of sixties counter-culture, while reminding us that the shadow always lurks – as does the oppressive reaction to pulling out bricks from the wall of convention.

As you get better at harnessing freak power, your success *will* get weirder – in the best way possible. When you pull your success closer to weird, people will start offering you money to do cool things – things that are much closer to your essence.

That resonates because it stems from the riddles of your identity. I call that creating your own credentials. That's what everyone from Lou Reed to Frida Kahlo to John Coltrane did.

Even if you don't take the financial offers that come your way, you can still draw on that freak power. I know bartenders who derive much of their existential joy from the bands they are in, or the clubs where they DJ.

They may never make any real money from those gigs, but in their subcultures, they have respect and social standing. Others are drawn to the charisma of their manifestation. That brings friends and yeah, social opportunity. Think that makes the financial gymnastics worth it?

Freak power isn't something you chase – it's just a potent byproduct of the cultivation of the creative weird.

Creative manifestation leads to taking up space, which leads to freak power. Turning your back on that is self-betrayal.

Do NOT betray yourself, even if others have betrayed you. Prove it to us: you are more than the abuse and disappointments you have suffered.

Whether that power leads to financial returns is the open question. Sometimes it will; sometimes it won't. Sometimes you won't need it to. But that's a good problem to have – figuring out what needs to monetize, what to give away, and how to make it all work.

Once you have your freak power, you have your audience. *Then your success should be weird enough.* Pursue the brazen adventure you always feared. If you're like me, the fear in your gut won't go away, but it won't stop you either.

This internally ruthless pursuit burns the entitlement right out of you. You'll be humbled by your own emotional resistance.

Taking that out on other people is not acceptable. It's a wrong you strive to avoid – not by repressing your rage, but by fusing it to the proper creative outlet.

In my world, intelligent rage is the sexiest quality imaginable – but only if it is controlled. It must be directed at the right things. Surrender it to the alchemist, along with the despair and the loss and the moments of beauty you've been lucky enough to experience.

Don't repress or deny this crazy mess of brokenness. As Metallica exhorted us, "Show your scars!" Don't try to stitch yourself into normal like I tried to do – you'll never fit that particular suit anyhow.

Face the Truth with Asher Lev – and Find Your Flow

Chaim Potok authored some famous books, like *The Chosen*. A lesser-known Potok title called *My Name is Asher Lev* is on your reading list now (slightly overdue thanks to high school English teacher Ms. Gronberg for that one!). *Asher Lev* is about a young Hasidic Jew whose artistic development puts him in conflict with his family, and the Hasidic values they espouse.

There is no requirement your art must divorce you from whoever you love, BUT: the kind of expression we are after means all assumptions are thrown into question. In college, I sent my father a poetry project that dissected men's relationships with their fathers.

One of the poems, "I divorce you," was a child's indignation against emotional manipulation, a satirical and somewhat playful line in the sand. Unfortunately, my father took it as a real line in the sand; we never spoke again. It was not the outcome I wanted, but I could no longer live in silent submission to his authority.

Yes, some comedies get away with a lighter approach to identity, but as a rule, the kind of creative work you are after has an edge

There's nothing you can do about achieving greatness in the eyes of others. Greatness in your own eyes is another matter. Maybe you can transcend your circumstance through art – if only for a few precious moments of flow.

The notion of "flow" harkens back to another book to dig into, *Flow: The Psychology of Optimal Experience*, by Mihaly Csikszentmihalyi. *Flow* is a landmark book analyzing optimal mental states, and how to achieve them – including peak states of creativity.

The way I see it, flow goes well beyond creativity; it's about cultivating a type of consciousness where you feel a connecting thread, a kind of egoless absorption with the rhythm of your life.

I think of flow as an ideal of how our lives can be – *if we can dissipate the conflicts between our creative soul and our careers.* Being "in the flow" is an aspirational way to live – and deceptively hard to accomplish.

To achieve that, you may need to pull an Asher Lev. You may need to move beyond your family's values (or your religion, community, or country). *You may have to risk exile to find your true home.*

You may be compelled to express controversial or obscene thoughts – and they may conflict with the perceived correctness of your community. Be prepared to lose those who are attached to the skin you are shedding. But when you move beyond, you find a different kind of comradery – including those throughout history who questioned their constraints.

Solace is just one brilliant biography away. If you're not sure where to start, *The Autobiography of Malcolm X* is an all-time transformation-under-duress story. Maya Angelou's *I Know Why the Caged Bird Sings* has a way of burning the excuses right out of you. Stephen King's *On Writing* is comparatively lighter fare, though no less instructional.

The confederacy of freaks on a similar path – you'll have their respect. No, that's not the same as friendship, but it's fuel you can use. And: friendships will stem from it. The only way to earn that respect is through the gristle you forged into art – regardless of consequence.

No Excuses – Punk Rock Your Way Forward

Too many wannabe artists are afflicted by a stifling perfectionism that leads to creative paralysis. Perfectionism disrupts your content pipeline; now your plans are pipe dreams.

One culprit: intimidation by brilliance. We've all read shattering books; we've witnessed performers whose stagecraft humbled us. That should never prevent us from pushing forward, in our own flawed way.

Punk rock your way to success instead. Go back to the early days of countless rock bands, punk and otherwise. Guys and gals who banged on their instruments when they could barely strum. They got better in the doing. Did they intend to become masters of their craft? Probably not. But they had something to say – and a drive to defy.

So they plugged in, and played their asses off. Whether it's The Sex Pistols or The Ramones or The Runaways – the joy of the jam and an attitude of disruption took precedence over fine craftsmanship. Usually, the craftsmanship catches up.

For musicians, self-produced YouTube videos might be the starting point. For the filmmaker, a "found footage" video in the style of *The Blair Witch Project* might be the way forward. It's all about minimal equipment, and even more minimal fundraising.

Writers can now self-publish short stories on Amazon/Kindle. For the comedian, "open mikes" are everywhere. Expose your material to a public gut check; do it often.

Kickstarter campaigns have their place – so does investing in the right equipment. But technical barriers are overrated. The launch is *way* cheaper than you think. That's the punk rock style.

This applies to software/app building also. If you lean in that direction, you know about open source communities like Github and Stack Overflow. The latest wave of tech startups are fueled by a "minimum viable product" method, where you are better off releasing a basic-but-intuitive app, pulling in feedback, and improving the software in an iterative style. So-called "lean" and "agile" methods provide a framework for this. You may find reading up and lean and agile techniques helps your creative projects – it does for me.

Or – you can cling to artistic tradition, polish a couple of chapters, send out the query letters and sit on your ass for half a year. Maybe you'll get a bite. I've been there – what a colossal time suck. Build an audience instead, brick by brick – that's no time waste at all.

The agent or publisher you seek will check if you've built that "platform" I've been harping on. Platform, in this context, is a wonky way of saying: you have a pre-established audience eager to consume your content, whether it's a YouTube subscriber base, a track record of appearing in fiction compilations, or a lively herd of Patreon supporters.

That platform is largely built through content sharing. Platforms thrive on the punk rock method of releasing imperfect content as your audience grows (e.g., a blog platform like Substack that builds a growing email list). Ideally, part of your platform includes data you own (like email addresses), but any public following will aid your cause.

Agents have an annoying/predictable habit of showing up AFTER you're already famous. Agents want to broker deals with those who are already "made," or close enough that they can smell the benediction.

If you want a taste of what I'm railing against, go pick up a "breaking into publishing" book. You'll read all about "writing a good query letter," and how to look up the right agent for your material. Toss that shop-worn playbook and write!

In rare cases, it *does* make sense to work with an agent; usually when one falls in your lap. But even then, do NOT stop creating. Get into a rhythm of creating and sharing, building your industry contacts as they react.

Phooey to these gatekeepers and their agendas about what is marketable. They're putting all the launch risk on you – so don't wait on them to bestow status.

Dr. Seuss was rejected. Agatha Christie was continually rejected for five years – then a publisher saw fit to give her a chance. Before Stephen King was Stephen King, a publisher said this about *Carrie:* "*We are not interested in science fiction which deals with negative utopias.*"

King never stopped writing (though rumor is he threw a draft of *Carrie* in the trash. His wife salvaged it). I'd say that worked out. Then there's JK Rowling, who garnered multiple rejection letters prior to a wee project known as Harry Potter (though I'm not a fan of how she's conducted herself on transgender issues, but that's another story). The moral: press the heck on.

Anything that gets you in front of your audience is the way to go. Anything that postpones the stage through expensive or time-consuming hoop-jumping should be shunned.

Don't fall prey to the social media confessional. Don't put every brain fart in the public domain. Put the promising but imperfect stuff out there; scrub as you go. My retired former colleague Den Howlett has a disarming mantra: "Suck less every day." This is how you do it.

My perfectionism is mitigated by a daily blog ritual. I've been forced to release work into the wild, accept its imperfections, deal with the feedback, and push on. There is an odd liberation to letting go of over-polish. Yes, I'm sitting on this book until it's as good as I can scrub it. But it's still going to be flawed. That's the punk rock way. I think you'll find it's your best way also.

Degrees Don't Make Your Art – Punk Rock Your Learning Too

Being a great artist isn't just about the craft. It's about having a big world and a questioning mind. It's about intimate knowledge of your domain. When your worldview is myopic, your creative potential is constrained. But as I've preached, artists and school don't usually mix.

You should be creating, not scraping through the mind crust of exam prep. School isn't necessarily bad for artists, but diminishing returns hit faster than say, for a scientist or mathematician, where a PhD program might be the key to advancement.

Artists who aren't in school make an altogether different mistake: losing track of intellectual growth. Just because you avoided the credentials trap doesn't mean you should fling yourself into a slack-jawed, Netflix-and-chill abyss.

I urged a punk rock approach to creativity. *Now you need a punk rock approach to learning.* Perfect the art of learning on the fly.

I take online courses from sites like Lynda.com. There are tons of free talks on YouTube. On long walks, I've got my audiobooks going.

Back in high school, I got exposed to a concept called "praxis." It's an out-of-fashion Marxist term that speaks to the integration of theory and practice.

The best way to learn is to consume small chunks of knowledge, apply them, screw up, refine, and seek further instruction. Integration of theory and practice gives your work depth.

As you pursue continuous learning, become a content curator. Curation, in this context, is the practice of filtering and recommending content to a relevant audience.

Curation is a Creative Discipline

With the glut of information, humans who sort and share the best info matter. Why bother? Because you're doing the learning anyhow. Share as you go.

Once you're set up, the sharing is easy. As you (selectively!) share, you're deepening your network, generating goodwill along the way. That selective/ discerning part is how you become known as an expert – which never hurts.

Curation is an underrated part of the creative process. It connects you to kindreds, who will later amplify your own work. Now you're getting closer to that hard-won platform, and all you're doing is thoughtfully sharing what impacts you – ideally with a theme in mind.

How? Develop a curation system – instead of simply "liking" whatever flashes by you in the social flotsam.

Be more systematic in how you consume, tag, and share content. An effective curation system takes a bit of setup, but it's not hard.

What you need:

- A means of reading/consuming the best content on the web (RSS newsreader, email newsletters, social network streams, lists, or news apps).
- A way to tag and organize the content you are consuming (Pinboard, Evernote, Pocket, Instapaper).
- A way to share the best of that content with the big bad world (Buffer, Hootsuite, Dlvr.it).

For each step, there are multiple tools to test drive. I use an RSS newsreader for mine – the awesome paid version of Newsblur. Within Newsblur, I can quickly scour a thousand feeds - which I have prioritized into topics and relevance. Pocket is my sorting and tagging area these days – though I tag my tech content on a public Pinboard. Dlvr.it pushes it out on social platforms to my subscribers. Pocket and/or Evernote are used for archiving special stuff in its entirety. The tools evolve; backup as you go.

Curators manage three types of content:

- Content you will read but not save.
- Content you will tag in a system like Evernote. In some cases, you may publicly share that.
- Content you share with your networks. It helps

> if you become the expert in sharing a certain type of content, whether it's graphic design, memoir writing, or horror flicks.

When I share content, I tag, or "mention" the author, and link back where I can. Eventually, you may get to know these smart peeps, perhaps online, or perhaps at trade shows.

Degrees are overrated for artists, but continuing education is not. Nor are the relationships you form, spawned by social curation.

Put Social Media on a Diet – or It Will Hurt You Artistically

I've flagged the dangers of the social circus, but tactical question remain:

Does social media help or hurt you artistically?

Social networks are in your face for the duration, luring you with their addictive charms – whether those charms fall into the category of baby pics or booty calls.

Hypocrisy alert: I've conducted my share of "get the most out of social" workshops. The underlying reality: I'm disheartened by social media. The utopian online dream is over. Social media encourages limited attention spans, intellectual superficiality, GIFs instead of coherent thoughts, the viral circulation of inaccurate or outright fake news, and mob cruelty. It might throw elections also.

Social media isn't great for art either. When peeps are showing off their selfie sticks, kindergarten-caliber "Facebook Stories" and cathartic venting about crummy jobs, they are distracted. And when folks are distracted, they aren't consuming your art.

For those who aspire to be artists in that provocative/transformative way, we need people who are immersive. Immersion might only be as long as a five minute YouTube video or a prose poem, but we need immersive tendencies. Incessant notifications via social streams undermine that.

But there's a bigger risk – our own social dystopia. We get caught up in the drama, and projects fade. Yes, that risk existed long before Facebook. I recall friends who moved to big cities in pursuit of big dreams, only to get swept up in clubbing and gallery openings. They were now too cool to withdraw – and create something that matters. But social media ups the distraction ante considerably.

The social media cattle call *does* provide you with herd behavior to avoid. As I've alluded to, when others fail to protect their creative space, solitude becomes your competitive advantage. Therefore:

The spoils go to those who unplug.

Unplugging doesn't mean social boycott. As I confessed, I check Facebook daily, but I don't *live* there. Now that everyone is perpetually distracted, advance your game. Hole up in the pottery studio or the film editing room. Head to the late night cafe with laptop in tow, if you can still find such a thing.

Protecting your solitude isn't necessarily a solo flight. Deep work extends to band rehearsals. It includes sitting with a trusted collaborator and crafting prose, or plotting out comedy sketches.

I see "deep work" as the obsessive-but-Zen-like pursuit of your own muse. Prior to the pandemic, I wrote a good chunk of this book at the Northampton Brewery, surrounded by noisy patrons. BUT: my phone was usually off, my email was off, and I stayed the hell off Facebook.

Deep work is not just about creation. Research your trade, whether that's reading *Moby Dick*, analyzing *Mad Men* for character development, or scouring articles on forensic science to add realism to your script. Whatever stirs your intellectual drink.

- Reflection, research, and creation is the deep work cycle.
- Tag as you go; curate and share when you come up for air.

Cultivating a deep work routine isn't easy. You'll be tweaked by outside pressures, pinged by fussy friends who need stuff. I've already pushed the virtues of a filtering system to let the right things in – and block out the rest.

Unplugging and the Power of Deep Work

Cal Newport is right. A deep work rhythm won't just help your creative life. It will change your professional outlook.

Newport calls this "value productivity," a very different kind of productivity than processing emails and filing expense reports. As I blogged in "The career-defining consequences of value productivity":

> *"Any competitive advantage I've achieved in the last five years is directly tied to the creation of high-value content."*

In his "Study Hacks" blog, Newport wrote:

> *"It's not that task productivity lacks importance – it has saved me much stress – but I think value productivity is what will rule in an increasingly competitive knowledge economy."*

You need your own rhythm of unplugging, excavating, immersing/curating, and re-emergence. I mentioned "The spoils go to those who unplug." That phrase comes from a spicy little post of mine, via an obscure blog post Tumblr tore down years ago. As I wrote then:

> *"These days when I feel that 'I'm losing attention' vibe, I try to refocus inwardly instead. The question then becomes: what kind of unique contribution can I add to my field? How can I advance the conversation? Advancing the conversation helps to cut through the noise; you can only do it via careful listening, which becomes the fertile ground for your own original work... There's no better edge in the noise economy than the fierce protection of creative solitude."*

The brilliant upside of solitude is your secret. It redeems the loneliness you might feel when you head down your rabbit hole.

So what does this have to do with the social marketing the gurus preach? Do we abandon the social psychochatter entirely?

Nahhh – you just need "social objects." In 2007, on his "Gaping Void" blog, Hugh MacLeod coined the term. In his case, it was art on the back of business cards.

Folks need stuff to share. They need inspiring music, cool images, animated cartoons to distract and impress their peeps. They need "objects."

The "social objects" terminology blows open the definition of shareable content, pushing it well beyond a book or a podcast. A social object is anything you create that can be shared on digital channels. Pictures of said object (e.g., a sculpture or mural) also count.

While your pals are lifestreaming whatever is edible or cute or meowing, you're deep diving in the lab, or coding your industrious tail off. Then you figure out how to distribute those social objects. That's where your web site, a vital part of your so-called "platform," comes in. Post and link to your social objects there. Then you push those objects onto social channels, linking back to your home base wherever possible.

Some argue a web site can no longer be an effective home base, due to the throngs on Instagram and Facebook and so on. I couldn't disagree more. Yes, building your own site is harder, and it will never be everything – but it's something you own and control. That's about creative freedom, but it's also about control of your audience data. And I trust you to respect your audience and its data – much more than the data vampires, aka the social media aggregators.

Social Objects Want to Be Free – Put Them to Work

Think of "social" as your chance to do a director's commentary, a *Behind the Music* look into your creative process – including sketches and outtakes.

You're not trying to be a Kardashian (not if you're reading this particular book). Instead, venture into social to build community around your work. The gritty tussle of creating social objects sets you apart. Now, you have something compelling to share – when and if you so choose. Now, you have a substantial *something* that sets you apart from the bile of lazy lifestreaming without context. Now you've avoided the trap of the pseudo-creator, who wants attention without excavation.

Yes, I have an unapologetic bias here. But don't you think "make social objects first" beats the heck out of an attention-seeking, fraudulent high-school-cafeteria-popularity-contest social persona, without the expertise or creative output to support it.?

Just remember – social objects want to be free. Maybe you can get away with a short sign-up, or an email opt-in, but as we've said, digital is about ease of sharing. Whatever your monetization scheme, your social objects should be on the free/trial/sample part of that scheme. You can still tie it to monetization, such as the chance to subscribe to the entire series.

Yes, the social attention frenzy can bring you down. It's beyond irritating when you sweat over something great, share it, and get minimal reaction. Then you share something trivial, something you did half-assed, and tons of people share it. What the feck?

I've talked about attention as a continuum, not an absolute state. Thank goodness you don't need to reach everyone. Your social objects should fit into your master plan, which is to build a network of experts, trusted collaborators and players, otherwise known by the rancid term "influencers," in your chosen field.

Stick with a genre or style if you can. Build up a reputation in that context. That way, even if your "share" only reaches a few people this time around, you're still connecting with people who dig your interests. You're reaching people who have a stake in your field, not praying to the algorithmic gods for virality.

And: you're developing creative inventory you can use or repurpose later, even if it landed with a thud this time around. Polish it, re-use it, and flesh it out. Blogs become books; short stories become anthologies; songs become albums. All the while, you're building what we call "topic authority" – and topic authority can lead to paid gigs.

If your thing is lesbian detective fiction, share a free story in that genre. Same with a poetry podcast. From there, you can have links to eBooks for sale – along with free subscription options. Maybe you'll also have a Patreon-type donor option, or paid subscription for the full podcast feed. Always make sure there is a free way to sign up for updates, whether it's a monthly mailing list, or an email daily. One of my college pals, Jessamyn West, built a notable niche via a stylish, semi-regular newsletter to fellow librarians (and library nerds like me). When you speak to themes beyond your own self-promotion, it resonates. And guess what? The audience somehow comes along for that ride.

Artists always had to grow their networks, it's just that their handlers did the heavy lifting. Now it's down to you.

Don't geek out over how many times someone shares a story, or how many followers you picked up. Yes, it's good to analyze traffic and data. But – don't let it get you down either. The long game is the only social game worth playing.

Piracy Is Real – Don't Let It Break You

You may be hesitant to share free stuff due to piracy. If so, I don't blame you. Take photography – it's a beast for photographers to combat pirates, thieves, brain-dead copy-and-paste hacks, and now, generative AI that sucks up your content as "training data," usually without permission or compensation. Yes, there are workarounds, such as embedding logos into the images themselves. But the workarounds are not as ironclad as the determination to pirate. "Free" doesn't work so lovely when your name or web site isn't credited.

Some believe they don't lose any money from piracy. "The pirates wouldn't have paid for it anyway," this line of thinking goes, and "Piracy can be good publicity." Others counter that piracy hurts sales and branding.

Musicians paint a grimmer picture of diminished CD sales, and anemic royalties from streaming services like Spotify – made worse by unauthorized "rips" on YouTube, etc.

I'm not going to get too hung up on piracy stats here – I've heard all I need about the impact of piracy from musicians I trust. That said, Nelson Granados wrote on Forbes.com that:

> *"Rigorous academic studies estimate conservative losses in box office revenues and digital sales at about 10%, so more realistic estimates should be higher. A 2014 peer-reviewed study at Carnegie Mellon found that piracy prior to release leads to 19% additional box office losses relative to post-release piracy."*

As for my earlier contention that fans don't care, one study I saw on Digital Music News from 2017 indicated that 39 percent of Americans polled don't care that piracy is hurting artists. A 2017 piece on Howlernews.com noted that "Studies have shown that illegal downloads and file sharing can reduce music sales up to 30%."

In some cases, like pirated eBooks, the original authors have all author credits stripped out, thereby losing the last potential benefit of piracy: viral exposure. Even those who defend piracy must admit: when beats or words are ripped out without any artistic credit, then piracy has no perk to the initial creator.

Yes, you can find artists who claim to have benefitted from piracy, but the point is: it's largely out of your hands. Tactics used to "lock" content can piss off paying fans – and the savvier pirates break those locks with impunity. You have no choice but to address this in your creative strategy, and there's no easy fix. Your strategy for piracy will vary based on the genre of art you pursue, and your end game.

When I'm in a cynical mood, I say that musicians must turn into t-shirt salespeople, and writers must become consultants.

Thankfully, that's an overstatement, but bitter truth does lurk. Piracy is just one of many factors that curb the revenues from creative work.

The days when artists could be anti-societal punks while their handlers smoothed rough edges are gone. You'd have to be Dylan or Cobain to pull that off now. If you're indifferent to putting yourself out there, interacting with fans, and selling products, you may have a financial reckoning ahead – ironically, even if your work is popular. If that's not a bitter pill, I don't know what is.

Some can't stomach these activities. Fine – *make sure your work is freaking amazing.* Maybe you'll carry it off.

I don't see a contradiction. You can create fierce, uncompromising art and still be accessible to "fans." You don't have to be an ass-kissy shill to create social objects. Make your own calls here.

Make Your Own Social Media Rules

It drives me bonkers when marketing savants insist you "have to interact with your fans." You don't. It's a gosh darn choice. Your mission hasn't changed: wrestle your muse; share the fruits of that skirmish. But I won't lie either: the advantage goes to those who are accessible.

If your audience feels a connection to you; if you respond on Amazon or Facebook or Discord or what have you, they are more likely to become passionate advocates of your work.

The more controversial your work, the more it will attract insufferables, trolls, and ideologues. That's where blocking people comes in, not to mention turning off notifications. Yes, you can lemon-squeeze value from social, but that's your call. You *can* find success without it – as long as you have a digital presence. You may be able to escape social, but you can't avoid digital.

Miscellaneous gurus and "creativity coaches" claim social networking is essential to your marketing efforts. That's an overstatement. It *is* useful, but only if you have social objects to give away, or expertise to share. Social is the final piece. Rush into it, get yourself spoiled by adulation, and you'll be another empty vessel.

Let's say you're invited to a big industry event – heavy hitters with connections will be there.

If you don't know what you want out of life, such a shindig would be useless. But: if you just finished your first movie script, then meeting an agent, collaborator, or movie director at such a shindig might be useful, even serendipitous. Social is kind of like that party invite. *Don't come to the social party without clarity on who you are – and creative output to offer.*

It doesn't work to tease people anymore. Don't trickle out a thirty-second preview video, or glimpses from a book chapter. You must give away something of greater worth. *Give them a so-called "experience."*

Give away a few of your songs; let people stream your whole album for a limited time. I've mentioned how book authors might offer the first book in a series to build readership. Once readers are hooked, charging for the next book is more viable.

If you plan to charge for *all* of your art, at least make buying and consuming incredibly simple. That's what I mean by "frictionless consumption." Writers are able to charge for their work on Kindle because the buying/downloading experience is quick and easy – way different than the tedium of digging out a password and thumbing out a credit card. Asking people to type in a credit card through a clunky payment system on your own web site? That's not frictionless enough. At least offer PayPal or Google Pay, etc.

No hard and fast laws here. Break rules. Experiment. The biggest media publications in the world are trying to nail down profitability – what they can charge for, what they can't, how much to give away. You can tell by their intrusive newsletter pop-ups and turgidly aggressive autoplay videos they haven't figured it out. Welcome to the monetization riddle.

Find the Middle Ground Between Obscurity and Taylor Swift

There is *plenty* of middle ground between total obscurity and Taylor Swift. Reaching the right people enough of the time gets it done. One of my fav examples is Sleater Kinney. This female-led band emerged in the early 1990s from the riot grrrl movement, and made a hell of an imprint on the indie rock scene. Like many long-running bands, they took breaks, broke up, reunited, and are now producing new material. There was never a sense of compromising for fame in Sleater Kinney's music.

Strung Out, my choice for the greatest punk metal band of all time, pulled off a multi-decade career on the fringes of much more famous bands. They've opened for the likes of The Offspring, a good band in their own right. To my ears, Strung Out is the vastly superior band, but that's not the point. The Offspring sold gobs more records. The Offspring had knack for radio hits and sing-a-long catch phrases, but Strung

Out did their thing too. Even as they switched up their sound, Strung Out never lost their urgency.

The power of playing it their way emanates from Strung Out's music. All their records came out on the same independent west coast label, Fat Wreck Chords. Dig deeper into music history, and find The Velvet Underground, a band which managed to influence almost everyone, without ever sounding like they were playing for paychecks. The aforementioned jazz great Charlie Parker was far from the most famous jazz musician – but no serious jazz musician slept on Parker. In the *Jazz* documentary series, Keith David described Parker's gigs as follows:

> "*On the bandstand, Parker risked everything, furiously pouring out fresh ideas as if his very life depended on it. Shocking everyone who heard it with his speed, his fire, his ferocious concentration.*"

When someone says that about you, your legacy isn't shabby, fame or not. But you don't have to choose between being an artistic pioneer and being broke. As I do my final revisions, I have a playlist by The Cure running, an enduring band that always did things their way. With Robert Smith as the constant, they remain a commercial powerhouse.

Yes, there is a vanishing middle class of artists across disciplines, but there are sufficient examples of achieving "enough success" to know that it's possible – without the potential compromises inherent in chasing a bigger (and still uncertain) payday.

But you're gonna have to pull out the best damn work you know how. As Hugh Macleod put it on one of his classic illustrations: "*Quality isn't job one. Being totally fucking amazing is job one.*"

Yes, you'll need to scour web analytics to better understand what's working. And speaking of Macleod and his monster distribution list, you might need to build one of those too. Email still puts butts in seats (though texting is gaining steam). Speaking of which, when you decide where to build a subscriber base, prioritize those like Substack that let you export your data.

Don't blow gaskets if you have bad days on social media. Accessible – yes. Always on? No! Put those filters to work.

I keep more to myself than I used to. It's kind of a pushback against lifestreaming. Amidst an epidemic of compulsive over-sharing, mystery can be intriguing. Reject expectations; find your own balance. Not to mention, in an era of AI web scrapers, your public posts can become training data for AI engines like ChatGPT. Share carefully.

One more social danger to be wary of: the lure of instant validation. So many greats coped with the predicaments of obscurity. Herman Melville published *Moby Dick* to underwhelming response. He wrote a few other novels before taking up a career as a New York customs inspector. During his last thirty years, his work languished.

Melville wrote the occasional poem, but he was completely unaware of the stature Moby Dick would one day achieve. I don't know if Melville made peace with his obscurity; it seems he was able to carry on.

I'll never know, but I like to think of Melville as someone who balanced his personal ledger. He didn't know what his work would someday become, but he had a worthwhile self-confrontation, and emerged with work product – and lyrical grace to spare. Social media can't spare you from that necessary skirmish.

Scrape Deep – or Face the Creative Consequences

Before you construct a life around your art, before you consider a sacrifice proportional to your dreams, consider the soulfulness of your undertaking.

Not all our creations are created equal. Recently, I've taken confessionals from folks with enviable creative careers, at the level few ever reach. Yet they are haunted by books not written – truths they can't utter in the confines of their career.

We are meant to scrape deep. We might write product reviews for a living, but we really need to write about a high school friend lost to heroin. We write a sports column, but we need to write about the unknown parent who gave us up for adoption. We do wedding photography, but we need a format to express our gender fluidity. As the Sundance Channel recently put it, "No guts, no story."

It's about the type of success we want. Is it the kind we burn for, built from our own truth? Or is it a lemonade version we are then locked into? As I once wrote:

"You foresaw this.
I would build a mansion by the sea
just funky enough to pass inspection
and then, in the one act that might redeem me,
I would pay for my own destitution,
sleeping on the rabble of the
life I repudiated,
curled up near the wrecking ball."

Build inauthentic structures, and you might wind up like me, tearing them down and starting all over again. When you stick to that truth, you're positioning yourself for a sweeter success, and maybe a bigger one. There's something about art forged with a glorious indifference to commerce – it has a way of attracting money eventually. As long as you protect that incubator.

There are two semi-objective criteria for judging creative work that stand out:

1. How brilliant is it?
2. How original/unique is it?

There is, of course, an all-important third criteria – "does it resonate with me personally?" But that's an undeniably subjective response. For me, that will always be summed up by Stephen King's early epic, *The Stand*, which I consider to be the greatest novel ever written. By that I mean – it's my damn favorite. No, it's not *The Brothers Karamazov.* It's not even *The Idiot* or *Notes from Underground.* I admire the author of those three books, Fyodor Dostoevsky, in a way that dwarfs how I perceive King.

Dostoevsky earned that by surviving a death sentence, four years in a Siberian prison camp, and somehow finding a way to derive creative inspiration from his epileptic seizures, on the way to writing some of the most important novels in world history – without ever turning 60. As Albert Camus once wrote, and I paraphrase:

> *'I feel humility, in my heart of hearts, by only the greatest works of the imagination and the most abject poverty. In between the two is a society I find ludicrous.'*

I feel that same humility about Dostoevsky every time I read him. But *The Stand* moves me like no other. When I was a kid, *The Stand* transported me from a stifling Oklahoma bedroom to the dark possible. I'm not sure if I ever returned.

That's what counts, then – how did the work change us? Yes, there is a fourth criteria to consider, sheer entertainment value, and that counts also. (Entertainment isn't necessarily a superficial criteria;. the art of a good yarn isn't as easy to conjure as critics think, and less original, derivative art can still please audiences.)

When it comes to paying the bills, entertainment value vaults into first place. These criteria aren't necessarily in conflict – the best art typically entertains on one level, while provoking a deeper meaning. We want to be lured into immersion. Even better if we come out changed. We want to be emotionally affected, intellectually provoked. We want to feel better, or smarter, or provoked off our assumptions. Well, not everyone wants intellectual art; some want warm tapioca. Wrong book alert. But anyhow...

Creative perfection is so damn hard. We won't always nail the narrative. We won't always entertain. *But we can always be brave.* We can find the gristle in our soul. We might not be more famous, but we can sure as hell be more honest. We can ask:

How deep did we scrape? By "scrape" I am NOT talking about the intentional infliction of self-harm. Instead, pry open that foreboding door at the end of the hall. Empty that secret from the tiniest nook in your heart. Give us what lurks at the pit of your fears.

As for brilliance, well – we can't control the brilliance of our work. All we can do is pursue mastery with all the passion and longevity we can conjure. If we claw at our craft, taking unexpected risks as we hone, we've maximized our chances at brilliance.

The rest is beyond our control. The work we leave behind will be imperfect. It may occasionally flirt with lyrical perfection – or connect with people in ways we weren't expecting. It may even, on rare occasions, be exceptional.

We *can* control how deeply we scrape. Granted, not all of our work needs to go there. There is also a place for creative lightness and satire. But in the end, our work needs to open those last desperate doors.

Be forewarned: if you build your art on the comfortable omissions of convention, it will either blow up on you, or stalk your day-to-day, poisoning it with a pervasive sense of phony that no amount of material comforts – or prescription drugs for that matter – can remedy.

I'm not sure if I've ever enjoyed my career more than now, duking it out with my daily content. I don't try to fit in anymore. I just put as much attitude, craft, and expertise into tech blogging as I can.

But there are places tech blogging can't go – places I am haunted by. This book is one way to get closer. If I go weeks without pushing ahead on it, I get cranky and insufferable.

You're operating on two separate quality scales: the pursuit of excellence, and the pursuit of depth. The pursuit of depth makes your transparency more compelling. There is more to latch onto.

Forget perfection. People respond to imperfect work – *if* it is brave and authentic. Your technical brilliance is memorable, but your imperfect rawness is emotionally moving. Be aware of both quality scales. Then you'll know where your shortfall lies.

Think Quentin Tarantino – one of the most technically gifted directors of his generation. He's got ingenious films under his belt, including one that changed movie history, but how many deep scrapers? Yes, *Jackie Brown.* But for every *Jackie Brown*, he's got three or four riffy sendups like *Death Proof.*

Tarantino gets away with that. How? Through sheer technical virtuosity, a knack for a yarn, and a heaping helping of snappy dialogue. I'm not sure we can. And I'm not sure we're supposed to. *I think we're supposed to dig.*

What happens when a technical virtuoso digs? I think of Dire Strait's Mark Knopfler. Pick your solo – today I'll go with the staggering subtlety of "Brothers in Arms." I think of Pink Floyd's David Gilmour, issuing not one, but two of the most emotional (and emotionally controlled) guitar solos of all time in "Comfortably Numb." Or Slash, just 30 seconds into Guns N' Roses' "Estranged," taking the song into cult immortality with his guitar's lonely perfection.

I think of Joni Mitchell's *Blue*, one of the greatest albums ever recorded. *Blue*'s originality was palpable: it came out in 1971, just as a confessional style of solo singer-songwriter was emerging. But it was Mitchell's rare fusion of technical mastery, songwriting/vocal chops, and naked honesty that made the album. *Blue* oozes soul, but what is overlooked in all that cathartic lyrical purge is the discipline of craft. No, we probably won't achieve all those things in one piece of art, but Mitchell gave us one hell of a compass.

I wasn't old enough to see a young Joni Mitchell capture that on her guitar, but in 1991, I did see Tori Amos do astonishing things with the same radical authenticity, except on the piano – all for a five dollar cover at the Iron Horse in Northampton. That was my lucky view of her tour for the epic *Little Earthquakes*. To this day, Tori's "Silent All These Years" may cut closer to this book than any other song you can find.

Creativity is an Excavation

If you're lucky enough to land a creative gig, you can pursue mastery on the job. Getting paid to get better can't be beat. But your job will probably fall short on depth. Yes, force the issue if you can. Usually there are limitations on how naked (or outspoken) your employment can get.

I'll concede this: "Create work with authenticity" sounds kinda pretentious. Here's a less snotty version: you only have one go 'round. *Your work better be as absolutely unique as you are.* As I've preached, that means facing up to the buried parts of yourself. Friends you've shafted; sexual attractions that confuse you; addictions that take you right onto the ledge.

That's what your art wants you to confront, and, if you are lucky, transform – *but you have to go there.* You can eventually distance some of that authenticity as fiction – perhaps even utilizing a fiction writing pseudonym – but I believe you must confront it as truth first.

That means facing all the times you ran. That means staring into the volcano crater of everything you've lost. I have this jugular mantra:

"*Some of my best friends are happy. Some of my best friends are dead. And I'm here – today.*"

None of it makes fuck-all sense – except that today needs to be sculpted, before life does you. When you create something today, you honor those who fell. You atone a bit for those you shafted.

No, you won't win back those you've hurt. *But you may find solace in your art* – if you let it speak to what you cannot fix. Your art will push you into a different identity than the skin you wear now. It's a stronger you – more potent, less toxic. It's also more alone. It's more freakish and exposed, but in a less lonely way, if that makes any sense.

Artistic loneliness is doubting whether you have something unique to say, and burying your craft in the allure of addictive substances, or the quiet despair of getting by. Creative aloneness is accepting that finding your voice will set you apart.

From that place, you find connections. You opened up the space for them to spark; you carved yourself out. Now, ironically, you can aspire to be whole. You might not find many kindreds out there, but the ones you *do* find will change everything. Some of the best ones might be on your bookshelf, and yeah, maybe even on your Kindle. Those artistic swashbucklers from distant decades were always whispering in your ear. You just couldn't hear them – not until you placed a creative bet you can never walk back.

The struggle to create brings far more peace than ducking your talents ever did. Those who claim creativity is all light and joy – that's balderdash. Creativity is a reckoning.

On Political Activism, Self-Deception, and Art in Dangerous Times

Since I started this book, the political situation in the U.S. has become rather intense, to say the least. I have intentionally avoided the mention of politics in this book because art gets at elemental questions that go beyond politics. But where we've arrived at in the U.S. – and in many other countries, alas – is beyond left/right, into the specter of proto-fascism and/or a dangerously toxic media environment. In such times, artists must take positions too – and figure out how their art fits into those stances.

Repressive societies attack and diminish the role of artists – or they sanitize/sponsor their work as propaganda. Then there is the great dumbing down. See: network television.

Some believe that in times of political urgency, art is irrelevant, or even bourgeois. That same debate flared in the World War Two era, between the likes of Albert Camus and Jean-Paul Sartre (Camus thought art still had an essential place; Sartre felt it was a luxury distraction from the people's struggle at that time). I don't believe that art is ever irrelevant – but it's not omnipotent either.

You create because you burn to do so. The more depressing the political situation, the more potent art can be, as an antidote to the nihilism that lures us into the abyss.

Personally, I'm not a huge fan of blatantly activist art. Preaching tends to have a limited audience. Film director Stanley Kubrick once said, "The hard part of art isn't figuring out what to say. The hard part is burying it." The only problem is I can't find the quote, so either I screwed up, or it's not such a famous quote after all.

While digging for that quote, I came upon a relevant bit from filmmaker Edward Zwick:

> *"There is no reason why challenging themes and engaging stories have to be mutually exclusive – in fact, each can fuel the other. As a filmmaker, I want to entertain people first and foremost. If out of that comes a greater awareness and understanding of a time or a circumstance, then the hope is that change can happen."*

There are exceptions to the clunky vibe of most "activist art" – I think of the undermining cleverness of satirical cartoons, or Onion-like commentary. Same with documentaries. Otherwise, it's hard to do activist art that avoids the tone deaf curse of the heavy-handed.

Activism can be fueled by art, but the two are not the same. Art reaches hearts and minds in a way that argumentation cannot. But that's your call, not mine. You must choose the tone for each project. Switch it up whenever you see fit.

I'd be a fool to claim that art is more important than political protest, or civic actions like voting drives. But for some of us, there is an imperative to create. That doesn't go away – no matter who is abusing power around us, or how many protests we attend. Some of the best art ever made tackles those issues, from George Orwell's *1984* to Chinua Achebe's *Things Fall Apart*, from Zora Neale Hurston's *Their Eyes Were Watching God* to Ralph Ellison's *Invisible Man.* I'd add John Okada's *No-No Boy* to that list.

Never fall into the mental trap that art is a privilege for elites that must be cast aside in the interests of the struggle at hand. The best art reframes the struggle; it raises questions on who we want to destroy, and why. During the final stages of this book, I watched the exceptional TV show *Station Eleven* on HBO (I'm told the book is as good, if not better). It's instructive to see how, in this post-apocalyptic context, art is almost as important as food. Obviously, hunger comes first. But the hunger for meaning and inspiration isn't far behind. We need a narrative that gets us out of bed when all that lies ahead is dread or toil. Artists like you are driven to somehow provide that. It's not a burden to take lightly, but it's the most profanely sacred job I can think of.

In the era of trolling, vitriol, and the barbs that pass for discourse, your badass/thoughtful creativity is more important than ever. So get to it. Your art might not change regimes. But don't give smug assholes in power the satisfaction of your silence either.

During a wave of revisions, the #MeToo movement gathered steam, with previously respected artists like Louis CK or Garrison Keillor getting called out for hypocritical, abusive, and/or inappropriate behavior that casts an unflattering light on their careers.

Whether an artists' work can ever be separated from abhorrent behavior is a matter of debate. What I do know is this: at some point, you cross a line that trashes your own legacy.

Perhaps not every allegation has merit; I'm sure many of them do. They are still a wake-up call. We should confront ourselves early and often — before our success gives us a cowardly screen to hide behind.

The Necessary Redemption of Losing Your Illusions

That brings me to the HBO series *True Detective*, season one, a grizzly/mystical crime drama. Yep, spoilers (of a sort) ahead. If that's a problem, skip a page.

Our two male protagonists are filled with falsehoods – half-baked versions of themselves, masked by lies and addictions. The price they pay for that falsehood is steep.

Their strange redemption is found through the humility of losing (almost) everything. It's found through the intrepid, unconventional pursuit of truth. *It's found through a shift of mastered skills into a daring project of conviction, of mission, of obsession.*

On the other side: an odd-but-truthful success, buoyed by a tenuous peace with prior transgressions. The opening up from that accomplishment – perhaps their first proper/brave/soulful undertaking – allows for a bittersweet friendship between them, a spiritual connection with themselves and their families that had eluded them, buried in the bluster of a misleading, generic success, and tepid/problematic living on the back of unexplored places.

As you headlong into your creative unraveling, you too may feel an uncanny sense of destiny. You might catch a glimpse of that strange perfection.

For the last time: renounce the seductive pull of play-it-safe. Let go of the alluring comforts of a more conventional life. Then – and only then – will your art pull you where you crave to go.

If You Want to Make Big Art, Live a Big Life

I've refrained from offering advice on the one thing that is sacred: how you summon work to the page, or sculpt on your wheel. That is between you and your beyond. But I've implied this, so I might as well say it: *a big life helps your art.* I've talked about pushing intellectual boundaries via praxis, but that's only the seeds.

As much as I prattle on about mastery, sometimes the best thing an artist can do is jam possessions into a knapsack – and cross borders.

If you are broke or unable to travel, no matter. Invest your curiosity in thick, dusty books and mind-expanding exercises – err, I mean, mentors. Intellectual adventures count too.

Don't just live big; listen big. Cast a wide genre net in your creative consumption. Readers might be surprised to know, thanks to my mother's living room stereo, I grew up on women's music in our house, whether I wanted to or not. No, not Ani DiFranco; she came later. I mean the 70s days of genre-launching. I didn't like all of it, not by any means. Even back then, Ann and Nancy Wilson of Heart were more my style. But I'll put on Cris Williamson's historic *The Changer and the Changed* any day of the week. Something about Williamson's struggle to redefine informed my own. Guts and craft is a hard combo to resist. Consume widely – a cultural comfort zone can become a creative cesspool pretty quickly.

Push until you feel that *yikes* in your gut. No, it doesn't guarantee you'll make great art, but maybe you'll avoid the insular. Find what the punks call your straight edge. A literate, unflinching view of the world will propel your (sober) creative resistance.

Nothing wrong with writing an intimate memoir though! It's a matter of tone, not genre. There is a palpable difference between sharing a small part of a big world, versus writing about a small world with ignorance of the larger.

If you're torn between a summer of writing and a summer of teaching in Ghana, do Ghana now. Stash adventures in psychic drawers for future rummaging.

Art with big ideas and expansive worlds compensates for creative shortcomings. When Captain Ahab is boarding, you might want to be on his crew.

Don't Chase Love – Chase Your Muse Instead

It might seem odd to end this book on love, after extolling the virtues of freedom and creation. But I think in the end, most artists are looking for an exceptional kind of love – they just have a non-negotiable detour to get there.

Substitute love for the reckoning and you're screwed. If you don't believe me, take a paper cup, cut the hole out of the bottom, and pour yourself some water.

I hope the boldfaced lover you crave will see your creative light burning like a goddamn blow torch. I hope they are drawn to your flame above all others.

That's the one you want to find. *That means you must do anything to keep shining.*

They won't find you out of pity or compassion. They need to see your beacon splash across their sky. It's the act of external manifestation – and creative performance – that will draw the right people in (and, it must be said, a disconcerting amount of the wrong ones).

Like the flawed heroes in *True Detective*, we can learn from our failed attempts to erect a cookie cutter life. No more force-fitting relationships. Clear space. Create things no one but you can conjure. See who is drawn in.

But – you must say no before you say yes. If you don't find your no, life will force you to "no" via health breakdowns, divorces, lost jobs, and fortune-changing accidents – these are the strange gifts that set us on our path.

Broach peace with your predicament, and your solitude. Then you can let the right kind of love in – or not. Sometimes, that solitary path into the deep woods is all there is. And that must be enough.

The Wrap – Buy Your Ticket, and Ride It Out

Once you've accepted the glorious/terrible price of your ticket, all that's left is the fine print:

- What you want to say,
- The medium you will master,
- How you're going to fund it, and
- How you will sustain it.

The creative economy is either a character-forger, or a spank tunnel. Most times, it's both. But these methods of last resort should help. Now to test and hone them:

Your uniqueness will inform your art – find it and claim it.

Hone your craft in a dogged pursuit of mastery.

Find a sustainable way to create art that is not accountable to commerce, or how you pay the rent.

That audacious/experimental art should be *in addition* to whatever you create for pay. Incubate that fragile work until your voice holds; build up an inventory of edgy creations to mine and polish.

Don't wait for agents or funding – share work as you go, refined by the feedback loop.

Build opt-in audiences across your chosen platforms, signing up "fans" of your work who want to hear from you.

Become an active curator in your field.

Avail yourself of continuing education in any form you can. Self-educate into a bigger world to steep your art in.

Keep pushing towards the "weird" in your profession, and even more so in your art. Make sure your success is weird enough, or you'll be trapped in it.

Log as many exterior (and interior) adventures as you can. Jolt yourself out of comfort – until it becomes a habit.

Invest in the tools of your chosen modality as you go, avoiding lump sum barriers that stop you from creating. Live lean and fund your own art. Crowdfund if needed.

Resist the social media popularity contest – instead, immerse yourself in the "deep work" cycle of reflection, research, curation and creation.

Invest in your own web site which you own and control. That is usually your "hub." Choose your "spokes" carefully – they are the select social media sites where your audience hangs out. Extend your web community to those sites as well.

Punk rock your way from project to imperfect project as your skills and audience grow.

If you get stuck or can't find the time, pare down something else. Keep paring down until the groove is found.

That's it – rinse/repeat. Be a brave and terrified badass.

Even when you're caught in the time suck with no time to create, you can still do something. I call it advancing your cause. Each day, no matter the muck in your gears, do something to advance.

When you're advancing the cause, you don't just pay today's bills – you organize files and clear clutter. Next time, you'll do bills faster.

Cook soup you can eat for a week. Download audio books for walking the pooch. *Advance your cause, every day – no matter how ludicrous your obligations.* It's not as good as claiming time for creativity, but it counts. As long as you can steal enough time. A little here, a little there. Persist.

Eventually, you'll wind up with finished work for all that fussy toil. Once you figure out the right digital formula for what to give away and what to sell, you're on the way. As preached here, always err on the side of building an audience first.

You don't have to hole up in an ice cave on the Antarctic Peninsula to pull this off. Create amidst the fray.

The kicker is figuring out what your 9 to 5 will be. Tricky questions:

- How much art can you create on the job?
- How much does that job pay? Is it a gutbuster that saps your energy?

- How fulfilling is that 9 to 5?
- Does your work follow you home and eat up your free time?
- Does the job further your creative interests?
- Are you stockpiling enough to fund your art?

My family spent a lot of time gathering nuts. I thought they left some living on the table. I fashioned my life as edgier; I didn't sweat the nut-gathering. Not the most brilliant stance.

You too will need to replenish. You'll need a way to nurse your wounds, make peace with what didn't work. It's hard to stick the landing, folks. Happy endings are lovely. But you can write a hell of a story without one.

You were born with burning questions; they are yours to carry. The seeds of your fate are in there too. Someday, amidst your detractors, you'll find a way to plant them. And somewhere out there, typing in a tiny Internet cafe, I am rooting for you.

Epilogue 1 –
The Impact of the Pandemic, and AI

As I do the spit-and-polish on this ten year project, we're now in February 2021. It's another lovely day in the pandemic economy, with several coronavirus vaccines on the way. Amidst obsessive revisions, I conducted online workshops with Hampshire College students. Those sessions confronted me with what young artists are up against.

Another threat bears down on artists: so-called artificial intelligence, or AI. This falls within my tech blogging purview, so I should address it before I send you on your way.

The pandemic accelerated the digital shifts in this book. About five years ago, a friend of mine argued that artists will return to the patron economy. That phrase recalls a day when kings and lords commissioned artists for creativity on demand.

Perhaps a few artists will be underwritten by deep-pocketed benefactors, but we're clearly in the Patreon economy, not the patron economy. Patreon may not emerge as the dominant platform, but you get my drift.

In a gut-punch twist, writing in late night cafes might be one of the few things that doesn't come back. I don't have it in me to change my cover photo on the back. Think of it not as a nostalgic image, but as a prayer.

While I was hunkered down, an important book came out: *The Death of the Artist: How Creators Are Struggling to Survive in the Age of Billionaires and Big Tech*, by William Deresiewicz (July 2020). I'm sympathetic to Deresiewicz's stances – in particular his disciplined pushback against the Internet-changes-everything krishnas who fetishize creative opportunities. It's always the content aggregators that find a way to cash in – on the backs of creators.

Deresiewicz does a far better job than I of illuminating art-as-a-job, including all the production workers – also deserving of paychecks – overlooked by those who feel entitled to consume art for free. I agree with Deresiewicz: artists deserve to be paid for their work. Hopefully, his book will motivate us to push for changes in creative compensation.

Agents and editors aren't dirty words. I'm not demonizing curated media, or their gatekeepers. I'm saying: don't wait for them to bestow good fortune upon you.

My book is for a narrower audience. I'm writing for those who burn to create – those who struggle to manifest their art in a sustainable way.

That's why I support the organizations Deresiewicz cites, including WAGE (Working Artists and the Greater Economy). WAGE's push to establish minimum payment standards for artists, while addressing structural inequalities, hits the mark

However: I've been (self)burned by postponing my own art until such change arrives. I now take a different stance: work for change as you go, but never stop creating. Until that change comes, you need to outwit, outplay, and outlast. Whether you get paid for your art, or for the merchandise around your art, or for teaching your trade – those are personal/tactical decisions.

One thing you never want do: undercut other artists for paid gigs, via a reverse-auction race to the bottom. That's where WAGE's efforts to establish industry guidelines, which they call WAGENCY, comes in. I hope when you finish my book, you'll consider buying Deresiewicz's – and acting on it.

Before presstime (can't believe I can finally type this!), I became aware of another important book, *Chokepoint Capitalism: How Big Tech and Big Content Captured Creative Labor Markets and How We'll Win Them Back*, by Cory Doctorow and Rebecca Giblin. The book is similar to Deresiewicz's, in this respect: both books argue for structural changes, and point to systemic flaws that hurt artists. Doctorow and Giblin make a case for how we can change that. If it inspires you to act, they've accomplished their goal – but whatever your views, don't let the depth of these problems get you down.

I believe those who are blessed/cursed with creative drive have no choice but to press on. Compensation or not, fair or not, our creative silence will eat us alive.

If we were in a prison cell, we wouldn't stop. I think of Malcolm X, who transformed while incarcerated. He sensed what he needed to become. The energy behind that change was electrifying.

Behind bars, Malcolm X taught himself to read and write, hand-copying each page of the dictionary, diligently pronouncing each word, memorizing their definitions. In *The Autobiography of Malcolm X*, he wrote:

> *"As my word-base broadened, I could for the first time pick up a book and read and now begin to understand what the book was saying. Anyone who has read a great deal can imagine the new world that opened… I never had been so truly free in my life."*

That's why I didn't write a book decrying the digital economy. I envisioned a subversive guide to creative alchemy instead. This book is self-published because I want every goddamn word to be the exact word I wanted. I also wanted control on pricing. This book is free because I want no barriers for those who are drawn to it.

I've been advised *not* to price this book for free. I've been told readers won't take the content in a free book seriously. I don't believe that, but I'm about to find out. (In rare cases, I'll charge for this book, such as a printed copy, in which case I'll charge enough to cover the printing. Also, Amazon doesn't typically allow you to price Kindle editions for free, so this book will be as cheap as Amazon will let me price it – 99 cents is the goal).

Take digital power back from the algorithmic overlords. Build your own subscription audience. Then, perhaps, the so-called Patreon economy can actually work for you. The last thing we need is another empty Internet promise.

During the pandemic, a few clever/lucky artists reached audiences of digital consumers stuck at home, surfing for something better than the myopic news cycle. The rise of music reaction stars demonstrates the power of connecting with your audience. They figured out how to reach viewers in transparent, even vulnerable ways.

Their visceral reactions to music we love can be fascinating. And a reminder: communities built by authenticity can be a bigger draw than polished craft. Ultimately, we need all three. We need the unvarnished; we need the audience that springs up around that work, and then we need the craft.

I was struck by how the band Scars on 45 connected with their fans during the pandemic, via the intimacy of (paid) Zoom concerts – a gorgeous tonic against pandemic absurdity. In addition to live shows, Scars on

45 offered other perks, from merchandise to private one-on-one encores.

Scars on 45 marketed their online shows via social media, and their own email lists. Timothy "TJ" Leonard, the founder of CONNartists Concerts, acted as event facilitator. Leonard was a real asset to the Zoom shows, helping audience members with connection issues and handling requests. Scars on 45 wasn't able to tour, but they funded their recordings with these events. They found a way.

Then there is the problem of so-called "artificial intelligence." On a predictable basis, tech writers claim artists should be petrified by AI advancements. One writer claimed AI could provide you with the same noodling guitar solos Frank Zappa specialized in. Good luck conning Zappa fans with artificial substitutes. The same goes for text-generation, and machine-authored articles. Could a machine learn to author a formulaic genre novel someday? Perhaps, because you could teach a machine about the expected story arcs of that genre.

I hope I don't sound like a snob when I say that the romance genre is the most endangered by AI. But only the lowest-rung, most formulaic type of romance novels could hypothetically be generated this way – and that day won't be anytime soon.

Today's AI is not nearly sophisticated enough for that. Ask me again in 2030. Injecting soul into a book, honing the nuances of indelible characters – machines can't do that. Machines are incredibly good at a limited set of things. Tragically, algorithmic manipulation of our social feeds, and the propagation of misinformation at scale, happen to be two of those things.

Yes, machines are generating article copy right now, such as sports summaries or earnings call transcripts. I'd like to think you, dear reader, have excessively higher ambitions. Raise the creative bar; machines can't keep up. Do a search on *The Guardian* for "A robot wrote this entire article. Are you scared yet, human?" Then search out the rebuttal piece, "A human wrote this article. You shouldn't be scared of GPT-3."

GPT-3 is not the only text generator. But it has shaken up the debate, due to its relative sophistication. *The Guardian* wants to scare you with an article cobbled together by humans, from the best bits and pieces GPT-3 could crank out.

If anything, the artists' job is reversed: turn bits and pieces into rootable narratives. Machines can't do that yet, and they aren't close. Machines must be trained on large data sets. That's why robots are often better than humans at recognizing patterns across those data sets.

Do a search for "dogs" in your online photos sometime. The results are pretty impressive. But ask Siri to tell you a story about an abandoned golden retriever puppy, and see what happens. Come to think of it, a puppy can make up a better story than Siri.

Even with image recognition, machines have plenty of disconcerting failures. See the facial recognition and law enforcement debate – not to mention the persistent/embarrassing problem of bias against ethnic groups in pattern recognition. A recent search generated articles like "Facebook Apologizes After A.I. Puts 'Primates' Label on Video of Black Men" – by the *New York Times.*

For a decade or so, "AI" might be more of a help to artists than a hindrance. I put this entire book through Grammarly, weeded typos, flagged up crappy sentence structures, and (hopefully) gave you a better read. I also used Otter.ai's machine transcription service for book excerpts. In the push to publication, I decided, for the first time ever, to forego a human copy editor. Instead, I went with ProWritingAid's software to scour the book from another angle. But my budget remains the same – I'll be spending more on other types of humans instead (book design and audiobook production).

As I go to press, the bots are getting better. ChatGPT is the latest to inflame the debate, with proclamations that writer's jobs are endangered. Well, mediocre writer's jobs certainly are. ChatGPT can write a convincing paragraph, or maybe even a decent/flawed college essay. Maybe it's good enough for an academic crisis. But it doesn't change this simple truth: humans crave storytelling; they crave musical immersion. They crave something artistically that machines just aren't built to deliver.

I will concede this: I'm worried about AI's sophistication in image creation, after ingesting (in other words, stealing) the images of visual artists online. Visual art is so highly subjective, and the labor involved in creating visual art so intense, that I worry AI will encroach on the livelihoods of visual designers.

I still don't believe AI can achieve the sublime results of the best visual art, but for things like game design and character drawings, the bar is considerably lower. We must educate ourselves rigorously, and, when it makes sense, incorporate these tools to make our output better, or more efficient. Art is not in jeopardy, but: some of the remaining livelihoods artists rely on may well be.

Josh Bernoff, the writer behind the Without Bullshit web site, recently defined what human writers should aspire to. In his post, "ChatGPT: AI is now a decent writer. So you need to do better," Bernoff asked, "What makes writing worth doing?" His answer?

> *"Original insights. AI doesn't have those. Engaging prose. AI is weak on that. Wit. AI still lacks that."*

My adds:

> *A compelling storyline/narrative (fiction or non, AI sucks at that)*
>
> *Satire (AI can only guess at that)*
>
> *Subjectivity/honesty – inserting your own experience into your theoretical constructs.*

I have huge societal concerns about AI, including the aforementioned algorithms that dictate what content shows up in social feeds. Yes, that aspect of AI *does* affect artists profoundly. It affects who finds us. It affects our ability to be seen, and being seen is everything. Yes, if scam artists puke ChatGPT fiction all over Amazon, that makes our job of being seen that much harder. But I believe it also makes the craving for our profoundly human creations that much stronger. We just have to find a way to break through.

Chris Anderson wrote about the virtues of the long tail – people discovering weird niches (and, perhaps, unique art). Social media algorithms, which feed off virality, destroy the creative hope of the so-called long tail. The only exceptions might be work that is inflammatory, and thus socially viral. Tread carefully there.

Artists must dig into algorithmic life. Example #1: a new platform is aggressively featuring live stream poetry readings. You get in early, and gain algorithmic visibility. Example #2: you create a crime fiction podcast. Your next big job: getting listed in the right podcast directories, with the right keywords or genre categories. Garnering reviews is a big part of how creative visibility is algorithmically dictated. That's different, however, than AI creating art that rivals our own. Based on AI's current capabilities, that simply means our work sucks. We can push into something better; the robots can't follow.

As I've argued, the only exception might be visual art. Of all types of art, visual art might be the most subjective – and most easily generated by AI. Still, I think audiences can sense that indefinable soul, that imperfect truth humans fuse into craft. Look up the story of Jason Allen, an artist who won a Colorado art competition with "AI-generated" art, and the subsequent crapstorm. But when you peel it back, Allen spent 80 hours compiling and perfecting the imagery "AI" was credited for. Artists should grapple with these tools, experiment with them. I'm not sure they should fear them – yet.

As I polish the final revisions, lawsuits are pending that challenge how AI systems can "train" on copyrighted artwork. There are big, unresolved questions about "fair use" and "generative AI." This is a huge concern for everyone from visual artists to audio book narrators. We are in unprecedented times here. It doesn't mean stop creating. But it does call for professional back up plans.

When it comes to art-as-viable-occupation, I *am* worried about the digital economy. Who will fund in-depth investigative reporting, when the last remaining newspapers cater to viral page views and tight profit margins? How will immersive creators attract investors? If you get a chance, watch the documentary *Hearts of Darkness: A Filmmaker's Apocalypse*, about Francis Ford Coppola's harrowing adventures getting *Apocalypse Now* filmed (his wife, Eleanor Coppola, did a brilliant job on this unsparing film).

I can't imagine a movie of that subversive magnitude making it to the big screen today – not an auteur's take on Vietnam that's really about the epic themes of *Hearts of Darkness*. A unique one-off? Nah. If you can't present a plotline for *Apocalypse Now II: Mayhem in Miami*, you're not getting funded. *Spiderman's Sister Spins Webs* has better (franchise) chances.

My favorite director, the provocateur David Lynch, has made his final film. Lynch says there is no place for him in Hollywood today. (If you want to see uncompromising early work that gets it done without a massive production budget, check out Lynch's cult classic *Eraserhead* sometime).

That doesn't mean there's no way forward. Heck, Lynch could grab video cameras and crank out another harrowing low budget film. He's done it before.

Don't let the flawed creative marketplace define you. Invent radically different tactics. For a fantastical example of creative mastery by altering the use of time, watch/re-watch *Groundhog Day*. Bill Murray's character careens through a roller coaster of emotional states before the power of time finally dawns on him – as a means to hone character and creative excellence. In real life, of course, sledding is tougher.

That's the issue Hampshire College students challenged me on: *How do you sustain your art?* Burn yourself out, or back-burner into complacency – take your pick. Both lead to the same self-defeating place. But once you figure out that a modest amount of *consistent* time will fuel a basic level of creative output, the light bulbs go off.

I need to get this book off to print before new tech comes along. Now we have the phenomenon of

NFTs (Non-Fungible Tokens), and their potential to represent and validate digital assets, including art. NFT advocates are optimistic that NFTs can help prevent digital piracy.

I won't spend much time on NFTs here. I'm also not going to waste space with useless junk buzzwords like "the creator economy," metaverse, and Web3. You can probably guess how I feel about that hucksterism. I feel even worse when people fall for it, as if there is a lucrative creator economy waiting to hand us crypto tokens for light effort.

Yes, some artists are doing well with NFTs, including young artists who got into NFTs early. My view on tech: the shiny new toy really isn't. *Tech always cuts both ways.*

I recommend this attitude towards emerging tech like NFTs, the so-called metaverse, or anything else that comes along before I get this scrappy book out the door:

1. Evaluate new creative platforms carefully. There is often a big edge for early adopters, but that edge dulls quickly.
2. Experiment on the new platforms that appeal to you. Double down on the ones where you get traction.

Always look for the downside of any new tech. Never believe evangelical statements like "blockchains are immutable and can't be hacked," or "NFTs can't be stolen."

Epilogue 2 – Falling Short of Greatness, or Not

I spent the last three years trimming this book. Now, thanks to an unexpected confrontation with artistic greatness, I finally have something to add.

No matter how hard you burn for this, you may not succeed. Especially if you adhere to a narrow definition of success.

Your art may not succeed, but your life still can.

I believe you have two missions:

- Be the best freaking person you can be – day in, day out.
- Find and sustain a unique, creative response to your circumstance.

For artists, that creative response is obviously putting your work on canvas. That provocative act is, in itself, a statement against the mediocrity of getting-by.

"*Be the best freaking person you can be.*" It's the best protection against the whims of the marketplace. It carries you when the rejection letters come. I'm not going to tell you *how* to be that person – not when I'm still trying to decode it.

I'll say this much: when you start thinking of "love" NOT as something you hope to receive, but as a verb, a discipline, a way of paying a debt to those who risked for you – that's one hell of a starting point.

Our art will always be contaminated by our flaws. But that's different than using our art to prop up the powerful. I've studied the artists who took those short-cuts. They fell for money too extravagant to pass up. Other times, they became infatuated with the wrong things. They wound up with a corrupted legacy.

You must find the stones to question your own convictions, early and often. If you don't, you'll end up creating work for the status quo, which also lives inside yourself. It, too, must be overcome.

The dilemma, of course, is that few modern artists have achieved commercial harmony with unapologetically truthful work. That leads to all the turmoil we've documented here. It also lures us into the dangerously pleasant compromises of pseudo-success.

Creative role models who pulled it off are hard to come by. I've cited some of mine; you have yours. *But their glare can be too bright.*

That's the brutal thing about our creative heroes. They want nothing more than to inspire us into action. Yet we write ourselves off as failures by comparison. In some ways, maybe we have failed. But so have they.

I laid out the elements of mainstream commercial success to remind you:

When it comes to monetizing our work, there is a terrifyingly indifferent force of luck in play.

Taking this unfair circumstance personally is an occupational hazard.

You must somehow keep your faith amidst such daunting odds. You must keep that faith when your health is ailing. You must keep that faith even when it's in your nature to question it. Put your questions on the canvas.

History is filled with creators who lacked proper recognition in their lifetimes. The aforementioned Herman Melville, or the influential Danish existentialist philosopher Søren Kierkegaard, dying at 42 with no idea of his future impact. I think of the hugely accomplished poet Emily Dickinson, who battled eye problems in her 30s. From the Emily Dickinson museum web site:

"No discussion of the poet's health is complete without mentioning her increasing withdrawal from normal social situations, which began in her mid-twenties. Among Dickinson scholars, disagreement exists concerning whether hers was a deliberate choice as an artist to isolate herself so she could focus on her work or whether such unusual behavior as her startled flight from the doorbell, an increasing inability to see or visit friends, and speaking with select visitors from behind a darkened door rather than face to face, had a medical

origin, such as an anxiety condition. In any event, the poet and her family accommodated her unusual ways, which left strong marks on her poetry, including her desire not to publicly publish her poems during her lifetime."

Stories like this are closer to the rule than the exception. They lead us to only one conclusion:

Your adversity and your art are intertwined. Forget about unravelling it.

I am in the fortunate possession of a cassette tape I call *Dieselmeat 3,* a follow up to Dieselmeat's two obscure CDs from the early 90s. *Dieselmeat 3* has never been released, yet I'm perpetually astonished by its greatness. Sean Keefe, Dieselmeat's lead singer/ guitarist, once played in Gobblehoof, as did J Mascis of Dinosaur Jr. (though not at the same time). Mascis also played drums on "Deathwagon," which appeared on the first *Dieselmeat* record.

While in GobbleHoof, Sean toured with the likes of Bad Brains, Sonic Youth, and Nirvana. Meanwhile, Dieselmeat flirted with fame themselves, with rumors of a bigtime record label deal, and a six figure advance – signed and then lost. But the music lives – as do memories of stunning gigs in the glorious/notorious Northampton dive once known as the Bay State Hotel.

In my essay, "Remembering Dieselmeat: Reflections on Fate, Fame, and Unrequited Greatness," I wrote about the band's dissolution, and the effect that brush with greatness had on me.

I've battled it ever since – *that haunting sense I've missed the mark somehow.* I've been humbled by the colossal effort it takes to squeeze art into the margins of your life, when it's not generating enough income to put it in the center. Or: you fall sick while trying to keep it all afloat. I've tasted that bitter fruit many times.

The agony of cumulative disappointment leads to very dark places. But it can also lead you to an electrifying realization. Perhaps that friction, *perhaps that is how you were meant to live.*

That's the strange perfection you will resist – except for those moments of flow where it all sinks in.

In that Dieselmeat essay, I finally faced the truth:

> "*Long ago, seeing Sean play convinced me I would never become a rock star. The destruction of that dream was quite a favor, because behind that curtain, a different kind of stage loomed. And there was still a way for me to get there, if I could only get over myself.*
>
> *Whether I can ever do anything that compares with what Sean did remains to be seen. But I know that I do not mind dying trying. In fact, I plan on it. I used to think I was not for sale, but Sean showed me a further extreme. It was a maddening, vital lesson.*
>
> *As it turned out, the only hope for my creative redemption was to go there. I don't know what good can come from it. I assume that much of what comes next is not pleasant at all. But I can feel the fire of that commitment in my heart, and that is something. Sometimes, it is the only thing.*"

After Dieselmeat's near-brush with fame, and their subsequent crash-and-burn, Sean disappeared. He resurfaced on the west coast with a new band. But he was not the same. As I wrote:

> "*Daywalker, then, is a story of redemption, a story of finding love and conquering addiction. To keep his music alive, Sean had to shake the rock 'n' roll life. On another site, I found this mystical take on how Daywalker came to be: 'Friends and family died as the years slipped into obscurity. We found ourselves confronting our blackest fears. Somehow, our lack of traditional thought bestowed us with the ability to overcome the inevitable. We emerged into the uncertain light of day with a powerful knowledge.*'"

Yes. Don't coddle the many – save the few. God forbid you ever reach "the many" in an empty kind of way. If you do, you'll be expected to refill that soulless vessel until you resemble it. Imagine how many times Rupert Holmes had to regurgitate "The Pina Colada song" in front of expectant fans. Again to Daywalker. I wrote:

> "*If Sean was once willing to flirt with stardom and endure the drawbacks of mass marketing, he's not anymore. He seems determined to forge an alternative to the big nothing I call the 'advertainment monoculture.' On the path he's chosen, large-scale success is less important than turning a few people around. Some might prefer preening for music videos; Sean would rather carve out a safe haven for wanderers and outcasts.*"

And finally:

"*As Sean says of Daywalker shows, 'You can expect to see a group of people who understand your uneasiness in this world, while rocking your pants off. You'll see some misfits on a stage doing their best to dig below this happy, brainless veneer to expose the truth and beauty in pain. You'll be enveloped in our huge wall of sound and when you leave, hopefully, you'll feel better.*'"

Go find your personal Daywalker.

For decades, I've had a lifeline from Tennessee Williams scribbled on my wall. It reads:

"*The sort of life I had previous to this popular success was one that required endurance, a life of clawing and scraping across a sheer surface and holding on tight with raw fingers to every inch of rock higher than the one caught hold of before, but it was a good life, because it was the sort of life for which the human organism was created.*"

Early in my post-college forays, I knew a rough-and-tumble graphic designer named Phil. I'll never forget what Phil said to me, the same day he was fired. After getting the proverbial boot, he pulled me aside and said: "*See you at the top.*"

I loved his hubris in the face of a pink slip. I liked his implied comradery. Phil was wrong, though. *There is no top.* But there is a climb.

That climb is your perfection, and it is mine. I'll see you on the open cliff then, hanging in the breeze, the spark in our creative hearts somehow, unfathomably, intact. Defiant.

Jon Reed
Northampton, Massachusetts 2023

Book of Last Resort – Book Index

(key concepts, phrases, artists of note, and a few celebrities)

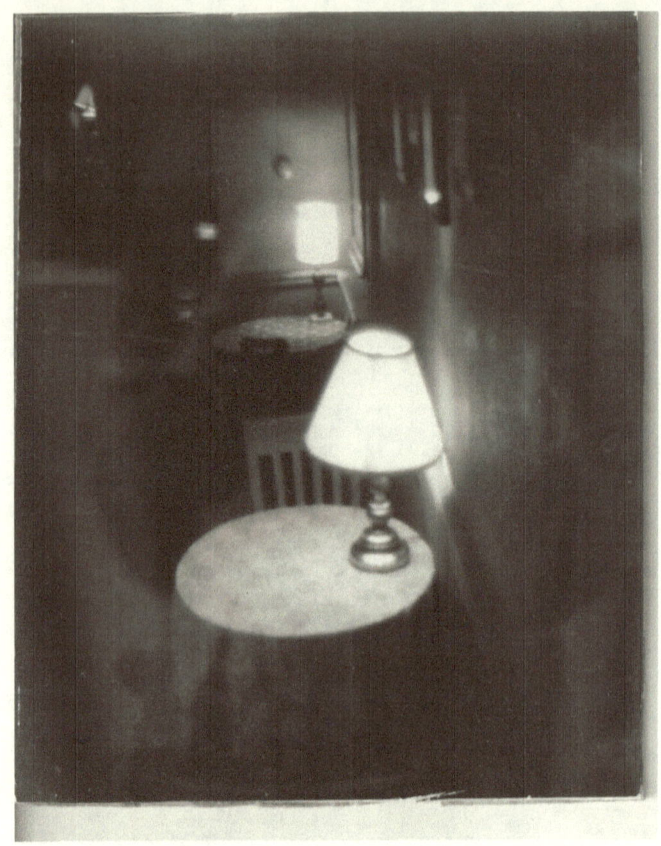

My favorite writing table – photo by Andrea Burns, Haymarket Café, Northampton, MA, 1994 (Also on back cover)

www.ingramcontent.com/pod-product-compliance
Lightning Source LLC
LaVergne TN
LVHW090936080826
845145LV00003B/774

* 9 7 8 0 9 7 2 5 9 8 8 7 3 *